Also by Jane Grayshon

In Times of Pain
Faith in Flames
Confessions of a Vicar's Wife
Vicar's Wife on the Move

A Pathway
through Pain

Jane Grayshon

Hodder & Stoughton

This edition first published in Great Britain 1995
based on text first publised by Kingsway 1987

10 9 8 7 6 5 4 3 2

British Library Cataloguing in Publication Data
A record for this book is available from the British Library

ISBN 0 340 634 47 7

Typeset by Hewer Text Composition Services, Edinburgh
Printed and bound in Great Britain by Cox & Wyman, Reading, Berks

Hodder and Stoughton Ltd
A Division of Hodder Headline PLC
338 Euston Road
London NW1 3BH

To all those who are hurting
somewhere inside

Your path led through the sea,
Your way through the mighty waters;
though your footprints were not seen.
(Psalm 77:19)

Contents

Contents

Introduction to second edition

Since this book was first published eight years ago I have received a constant stream of letters. People have written, not just to express gratitude but more significantly, to share a resounding sense of relief. 'Thank you for putting into words what I couldn't say for myself but I desperately needed to share!'

That is why I wrote this book. I am convinced that, even though we find it hard to say so, most of us have experienced moments of darkness, of feeling that prayer doesn't seem to be working properly for us. Many assume that they have 'too little faith', at least in the Church's eyes. Some also feel condemned by God; and in their disappointment and disillusionment they let go of even the thin thread of faith they may have had.

There are many books about Christians who prayed and were miraculously healed; there are others about those who prayed and died heroically.

Both give glory to God. They are thrilling testimonies which encourage us to pay attention to how God can act.

My pain wasn't miraculously healed, and nor did I die victoriously. This story is about praying and not seeing circumstances change. It is about being disappointed in God because He did not do what I wanted and asked Him to do. He was not obedient to me. Strangely it was in the acceptance of this reality that I gradually discovered that that made Him all the greater. He was God, not me. The sovereignty of God is painful indeed.

While I was preparing to work on this new edition I found myself turning, almost every morning, to Isaiah 61. This is a prophecy about what changes Jesus would bring to our lives. Jesus actually quoted these words when he first talked about the purpose of His coming:

> . . . the Lord has anointed me
> to preach good news to the poor . . .
> to bind up the broken-hearted,
> to proclaim freedom for the captives
> and release for the prisoners . . .
> to comfort all who mourn . . .

Almost every time I read the verses, I sensed a nudge from God. 'These are the people you're writing for!'

Thus I have written this book for people who are broken-hearted, captive to their circumstances, or grieving for what they have lost. I have written for those who feel poor emotionally, spiritually, or physically.

The reason I have written it is to convey the good

news that the spirit of despair, which naturally falls on us during times of deep suffering, need not stay with us for ever. We cannot shed the despair; neither can we manufacture a garment of praise. The good news is that God can do both – even if He doesn't change our actual circumstances.

I have written it because God doesn't always stop bad things happening. Freedom did not come from my pain. The beginning of freedom for me was to accept the fact that it looked entirely as if God had deserted me. That was when I began to realise that He is everywhere: even in our sense of abandonment. That was when I first glimpsed that He could be known in a special way because of the pain, awful though it was.

This is not a theological essay about 'the goodness of God amid suffering'. This book is about my search for the goodness of God, about not finding what I was looking for, but finding what I was not expecting.

Meister Eckhardt, a medieval mystic, wrote, 'God is like a person who clears His throat while hiding, and so gives Himself away.'

I hope in this book to share something of the reality of suffering, but also the reality of God whose cough we hear and whom we long to meet face to face.

JANE GRAYSHON
January 1995

Part 1

Overtaken by pain

1

'Let this cup pass from me'

(Matthew 26:39)

Life with three brothers had many challenges. Keeping up with them became my determined goal from an early age. It was very important to me that I should learn to survive their masculine teases without being labelled a sissy. We would all be told stories from the family archives about my grandmother and her eight brothers. They served to quicken the challenge I already felt. If she could survive eight brothers, then I would make sure I could keep my end up with just three.

'*You* can't go up our rope-ladder . . .'

'*You* couldn't climb to the top of the pear tree . . .'

I would rise to the bait every time. During my earliest years I decided never to give others the opportunity to label me a weakling. I would steel myself against any fear or pain; taking a huge breath I would climb the disputed pear tree. Inevitably I would endeavour to disregard those humiliating inconveniences, like bleeding knees or my ribbons falling out of my pigtails. On reaching the top I would feel exhilarated, if not by the view across to Liverpool then by the pleasure of proving myself – for that was how it seemed. To be acceptable I felt I had to be brave.

It has not come easily to me, therefore, to discover that there are situations with which I cannot cope. When all my 'bravery' was used up I have felt utterly unacceptable both to others or, perhaps more significantly, to myself.

It has been a rude awakening. Pain became a prominent thread in the tapestry of my life when I was twenty-one, creeping in like an intruder, a thief which stole a part of my very self. It drove me to the point of crying out in anguish, 'I can't bear any more!' During five dark months in 1980 I came closest to giving up altogether. I can never adequately describe the totality of my exhaustion with illness, with pain, with life itself.

In the February, when the crisis began, I was already profoundly weary from four years of chronic low-level pain. Though I knew it was normal for me, I still winced every time I moved too vigorously and felt the heavy ache. Pain-killers were either not strong enough or they caused me to feel sick. In any case, I tended not to take them as I feared that they would lose their effect if I took them too often. I dreaded having nothing to fall back on.

Pain began to be an unwelcome part of every conversation, so much so that I would secretly think, 'I hope this finishes soon; I need to rest.' Yet I couldn't rest, for the pain made me restless. And if I were left alone I would yearn for conversation, to distract me. Neither I nor my caring friends could win. There was no remedy. I easily became irritable, which in turn made me yet more irritable because I knew I was being short-tempered and I hated myself for it.

On top of this situation acute pain broke in. At first I thought I was pregnant. For two weeks my spirits rose, only dampened by the extra tiredness. But as the pain increased, my excitement faded. My experience of a few years as a midwife told me that my symptoms were ominous.

Somehow I managed to keep working. I cared for lots of patients who were complaining of pain, but inside I felt increasingly unsympathetic towards any who did not seem genuine. I caught a glimpse of one such girl giggling with her boyfriend in the waiting-room before she saw the consultant. Then suddenly, the minute she reached the consulting room, she looked very sorry for herself and she moaned dramatically of the 'terrible pain, doctor'. I was tempted to say, 'You've no idea what terrible pain is if you can giggle through it.' But I did not speak. One of the doctors for whom I worked was Richard, my own consultant. I was not ready to talk about myself – least of all to him. I suppose I knew too well what he might find if he examined me, and I was afraid. Afraid of being told I was not achieving my childhood aim of being brave.

Still, I kept going. Every evening I would drive home along the foggy Midlands roads and just flop into bed. Matthew was working so hard at college (he was training for full-time ministry) that he did not see how much time I spent in bed. He ate his meals in the theological college so he didn't realise that I wasn't cooking. At night he was so tired, he would sleep soundly through my hours spent vainly trying to find a comfortable position in which to sleep.

On one particular Tuesday I was unable to walk briskly around the wards. I had to collect a blood sample for research from a patient in labour. I remember the other midwife with me who was so comforting towards the patient. I found myself wishing that I were on the receiving end of such comfort. Instead I tried simply to keep going, keep going . . .

In everything I did, I had to give myself instructions.

'Walk over to pick up a syringe and needle. Force yourself. Walk over there. Keep upright.'

'Keep walking down this corridor. You can do it.'

'Smile to that person. Make your eyes smile as well so that they do not perceive how much pain you're in.'

The fighting part of my nature was determined not to give in. I thought if I ignored the pain it might all just resolve itself. If anyone had perceived the agony I was in and had asked me about it, I would have crumpled. In one way I longed for my pain to be noticed – yet at the same time I was terrified of what that might mean.

On the Wednesday I had to help with some medical students' exams. Normally I loved that, for I mercilessly teased all the consultants and professors who conducted the exams. I liked to pull them down a peg or two from the pompous stance they all assumed to terrify the medics. And they in their turn were so bored with examining, they enjoyed a bit of banter. I had quite a reputation for being fun.

But that Wednesday I was very subdued. At the end of the morning session, Richard was missing my usual drama and singing.

'You all right?' he asked quietly as we walked across an enclosed bridge for lunch. The door at the end was open, revealing tables laden with delicious food and girls in starched white hats ready to serve us generously. I thought I might vomit just at the sight of it.

'Not bad,' I replied, but my eyes didn't look at him.

'It's red for you, isn't it?' He gestured to the dozens of bottles of expensive wine. 'Oh look, they've even got your favourite: St Emilion.'

'No thanks, Richard. Er, I don't think I will today.' Richard looked at me incredulously and for the first time I dared to meet his gaze. 'I think perhaps I need some antibiotics.'

There. I'd said it. Surely I could be pleased with myself. And I could tell Matthew later that I had 'confessed', and he would be pleased and relieved. A few antibiotics would clear everything up. Wouldn't they?

Richard looked at me questioningly for a minute, then, needing to be involved with the other consultants and professors exchanging news of their recent researches, he agreed. 'OK. Get a 'script and I'll sign it.' He poured himself a full glass of Beaujolais Nouveau.

I slipped quietly out of the room. By now my abdomen felt as if it was on fire. I knew I should not have appeared so calm and composed in front of Richard. I should have asked him at a more appropriate time when he could have examined me properly. He always trusted me to ask, and this time I had deliberately made it difficult for him. I was too afraid. 'Never mind,' I consoled myself. 'The antibiotics will soon work.'

The afternoon passed. I longed to lie down or even to lean over a table and rest my head and my tummy. After he'd signed the prescription Richard looked up.

'You shouldn't be here,' he said. 'Get home and start chewing these.' He added a request for a huge bottle of strong pain-killers. 'You won't take these all at once, will you?' He laughed heartily at his joke. I gave a rather distant smile. I could not laugh, because even the muscular movement of laughter caused the pain to sear through me unbearably. In any case, perhaps it wasn't such a joke.

I did not go straight home. I went to my Sister's Office and wrote up all the outstanding reports, dealt with all correspondence and tidied up my files. I didn't want to leave until I knew everything was ordered and up-to-date. I must have sensed that I would not be there again for a long time.

I spent the following days in bed. Matthew's face became more and more anxious though he always tried to cheer me up whenever he brought me drinks. Every time he had to remove a tray of food I hadn't managed to eat, his face set a little more. He knew I was getting worse, but neither of us wanted to be the first to say so.

Two or three times we had to call the local doctor to see me. Once was on the Saturday evening and the doctor-on-call who came seemed so hard-pressed he appeared to resent having to come out to me at all.

'What can I do for you?' he asked curtly, getting

out his prescription pad and flicking his biro ready to write.

Matthew replied quickly, trying to save me from using my little energy on making explanations all over again. 'Well, four years ago she had her appendix out and since then . . .' he began.

'I am asking, what is the problem NOW?' The doctor twisted his pen impatiently, waiting to write.

I began to feel agitated. How could we avoid putting my present symptoms into the context of the last few years? This was no isolated dose of flu. I had not been completely healthy for the previous four years since, a few weeks after my appendix was removed in Edinburgh, an undiagnosed abscess had burst. It had poured its offensive, bug-ridden contents diffusely into my abdomen. Despite rigorous treatment by both surgery and by high doses of antibiotics, the resultant highly infectious micro-organisms were never completely eradicated. Every so often the inflammation reared its ugly head, each time bringing with it further debilitating illness and the possibility of grave consequences.

How could I summarise all that in one defensive sentence? Especially when the doctor sounded so pressured.

I was thankful that Matthew was acting as spokesman for me, because he still looked very calm. At the same time, he didn't know the shorthand language of the medical world and I wondered if I shouldn't step in with some jargon to make the doctor stop and think more wisely. I decided I must if we were to be helped at all.

'I've had pelvic inflammatory disease ever since,

with acute bouts of peritonitis intermittently. It seems to have flared up again now. I'm very sore.'

'Any pyrexia?'

'No, but my temperature hardly ever goes up even when I have a bad bout. We don't understand why not.'

The doctor had stopped listening as soon as I said 'No' and was back to poising his pen over the prescription pad.

'No pyrexia. Well there's nothing seriously wrong then. But I could give you some antibiotics if you really want.' He seemed pleased to be able to write something at last.

I looked helplessly towards Matthew. He often goes quiet when there's lots to say, as if he'll say nothing until he has sorted out all the thoughts that are clamouring in his mind. He stood thoughtfully, then his eyes met mine. I could see that he felt unable to argue against that great barrier, The Medical Profession. It annoyed me once again that doctors can set themselves up as if their opinion must not be disputed.

Fortunately, I was not left without an argument. 'Thank you for the prescription but actually I've been on antibiotics since Wednesday.'

'Oh?' He was slightly put off his stride, at least. 'Well, they should be doing the trick.'

'But they aren't and it's three and a half days now. I'm getting worse, not better. And I feel so nauseated I can hardly take them.'

He snapped his smart doctor's bag shut, lifted it off his knees and placed it on the floor. 'I'd better have a look at your tummy. Where is the pain?'

I pointed to the area over one side, carefully

avoiding touching it because it was so tender. He laid his cold hand on the opposite side and gradually worked his way across my abdomen, pressing as if he were securing postage stamps rather than palpating me gently. I pulled my legs up involuntarily and drew a deep breath.

Matthew jumped to my defence. 'Do be gentle. She's been through a lot,' he pleaded.

'This must be done,' was the short reply.

My hands were white from clenching my fists when he finished. I could not discuss things objectively now. Nausea swept over me in great waves but I was too shy to lean over the bowl in front of someone who made me feel so un-comforted. It would serve him right if I were sick on him, I thought uncharitably. But then the pain seared through me once again, round to my back and to the top of my legs. I closed my eyes to try to cope.

'I will change the prescription for different antibiotics.' The doctor picked up that wretched pad and biro once again. 'If there's no improvement by Monday, see your own GP.'

I opened my eyes a little. Matthew looked vaguely relieved. He must have thought this remedy was worth some respect. I could not share his confidence but for his sake I would do as I was told. In any case, what alternative did I have?

I mustered the energy to ask about what was bothering me. 'I feel so sick, I don't know that I can keep the antibiotics or the pain-killers down. I must have something . . .' I looked at him pleadingly.

'Here, take this.' The doctor rummaged in his black bag once again.

'What is it?' I never gave my patients any medicine without explaining what it was or how it worked, and I didn't intend to accept anything without knowing about it either.

'Just take it.' He held it out to me and nodded firmly before mumbling, 'You nurses are all the same.' His hardened eyes looked past me with little compassion and inside myself I shrivelled up. I was too weary to refuse. I took it.

After he had gone, everything became a blur. The mysterious pill made my head swim and it was hard for me to distinguish between what was real and what was only in my mind. My thoughts drifted around, accompanied by the fast throb of my heartbeat, almost like swirling music with a pounding drum in the background.

Matthew came and went, kneeling beside the bed and speaking softly and gently. His care soothed very much. I was so grateful, it was little cost for me to force myself to smile at him. But whenever I closed my eyes I was back in a world of pain. Sometimes I had nasty hallucinations, sometimes I sat bolt upright in bed or leaned over to try to shift the pain. Always I was aware of the pain.

On Monday morning, neither Matthew nor I had any doubt as to what we should do. After a quick phone call to an understanding secretary in the department where I worked, I had an appointment to see Richard immediately.

I do not know quite how I got myself together enough to reach the consulting room. Matthew drove me there, taking immense care to avoid bumps in the road so as not to jolt my tummy. The short flight of stairs loomed above me, a daunting hurdle. It was hard and I had to cling on to the banister for support but I made it independently, refusing Matthew's arm to help me up. Once again my age-old fear of being labelled a 'sissy' was taunting me. I mustn't be weak.

As Matthew held open the door of the department, my absolute terror of what Richard might decide about me was temporarily put to one side. Every thought I had was focused on keeping going.

I was back to programming myself. 'Walk, Jane. Just get to that chair there and lean on that. Be careful not to look as if you're doing a dramatic mimic of a patient in pain. Don't give any opportunity for others to think you're a fraud. Look normal. Don't stoop with the pain . . .'

I always tormented myself with thoughts that I may be taken as a fraud. I think this began when I was treated as one in Edinburgh when I first became ill in 1976. It was only one doctor, for one week, who was ultimately proved to have been completely mistaken; but his judgemental, sneering manner hurt so deeply that it echoed on and on. It's only now, eighteen years later, that I'm beginning to learn to switch off the tape of his voice playing in my mind. All through 1980 my dread was of being written off as not genuine. Rather than face that, I tried instead to underplay everything so that only a truly caring person – someone compassionate enough to look beneath the surface – could ever perceive how I was. It was a precarious game, keeping others at arm's length when what I craved most of all was tenderness and loving care.

Richard's distinctive step approaching jolted me. He beamed at us cheerfully. I swallowed hard and found a lump in my throat. I let go of Matthew's hand, wondering what else I was letting go of in the process . . . my fighting, my pretending that all was better than it was.

'See you down in the room,' he called to me as he whisked into the secretary's office to pick up my notes.

I set off walking ahead of him. He soon caught up with me. My progress was so slow, every step an act of will.

I thought I saw him glance down at my hand when I grasped involuntarily at my tummy whilst taking a step which reverberated through me. He would be getting suspicious. Had he also noticed how distracted I was? Would he guess why? I wished that I did not have to walk with him beside me. I felt extraordinarily vulnerable.

The corridor seemed endless, but at last I was in the examination room. With relief I almost fell into the black plastic chair to which Richard had gestured. I could not relax, though, lest my face should accidentally show the lines of contortion which I could feel inside me. I was still so afraid of him thinking I was a coward. I wanted to show my composure. I worked for the man: I didn't want to give him a reason to stop respecting me.

I answered his questions very briefly, almost curtly, for even the effort of speaking increased my discomfort; but I was honest. Having scribbled a few notes, Richard leaned over to take my pulse. There was silence as he counted.

He fiddled with his watch, his face puzzled. It was new: a fancy digital one from one of his lecturing trips abroad. Had he still not worked out how to use it, I wondered? I would normally have teased him that it was maybe too complicated for him, but today there was none of our usual light-hearted banter. I closed my eyes, sensing that I was beginning to take on the passive role of a patient. I felt I was being forced to face up to myself, to 'give in'. I couldn't overcome the pain either by fighting it or by ignoring it. It was overcoming me.

'A hundred and thirty-six?' The surprise in Richard's voice was mixed with obvious concern. After my being so accustomed to fighting for a doctor to take my condition seriously, I now did not quite know what to say. But Richard was not waiting for me to reply; he was counting once again.

'Your pulse is a hundred and thirty-six, Jane.' His face, normally rather mischievous with his dark moustache and huge dimple, was quite neutral. 'Bit high, isn't it?' His endeavours to remain unperturbed in front of me were countered by my seeing his pen circling my pulse rate strongly on my case notes. 'I'd better examine you.'

As I got on to the couch, raising my legs slowly to avoid any jerky movement jarring at my abdomen, I realised it was no use pretending any longer. I could have wept – but not just from the pain. My mind was totally confused, not knowing whether to be relieved that at last I was being seen as I really was, or to be afraid of the seriousness of my situation. Physical pain and emotional distress form a potent and destructive partnership.

After he had finished, Richard straightened his arms and leaned the palms of his hands on the couch.

'You know what this means, don't you?' It was more of a statement than a question. I opened my mouth to speak, but my voice wouldn't work. 'I'll book theatre for you to be done at 7.00 p.m.' I looked at the wall-clock: 5.00 p.m. 'But I'll make sure the ward is ready to receive you immediately.'

He shuffled slightly. He knew me well enough to know I liked people to come straight to the point, instead of waffling around a subject – and he would also know that given half a chance I would have questioned and disputed everything.

'Hang on!' I cleared my throat. I could see he was resolute, but my mind was still full of questions. 'What do you think it is?'

'Maybe an ectopic. You have all the signs.'

I gazed towards the empty gloss-painted wall. So . . . maybe I had been pregnant after all, but the baby was in my Fallopian tube. For some reason I did not feel sorry for this baby as I did when I nursed other women with ectopics. Instead, I was full of regret that I hadn't enjoyed all the glee of a first pregnancy.

Matthew would have been delighted, and so proud of me. I would have borne my parents' first grandchild – and me their only daughter among three sons. They would have been thrilled: my mother because she and I could have enjoyed the unique relationship of a mother and her expectant daughter, and my father in a different way. 'My darling daughter,' he used to call me.

And I would have loved the pregnancy, proud as punch. I'd have made sure I looked elegant in pretty dresses and I'd have relished this time of being eminently female.

These thoughts flashed across my mind within seconds. All this had suddenly become impossible.

The implications were far-reaching. The previous June, during another emergency operation, Richard had had to remove one ovary and Fallopian tube. If this was an ectopic pregnancy now, it was in my only remaining Fallopian tube. Once this other side had been removed, as Richard was possibly going to do in two hours, then I would no longer be able to have a baby. I was not only saying goodbye to my first, but to my only possible pregnancy.

I turned my mind away from such an idea. 'What if it's not an ectopic?' My voice lacked my usual vivacity.

'Then I'll have to open you up to see what it is.' Richard was certainly not going to budge an inch. 'See you in theatre,' he said firmly.

Back in the department I could not avoid being seen by others on the staff – my friends. Even with the supposed 'security' of being taken seriously by Richard, I still could not allow myself to trust anyone else enough to indicate that I was in great pain. Fear continued to taunt me: in two hours I might be found to have nothing much wrong, in which case I would be proved to have been complaining about nothing. Only sissies did that. Rather than risk such a horrifying label, I put on my act yet again, looking cheerful and saying airily, 'Oh! I'm off for another operation, folks. Unzipping me again!' And they laughed, as my words suggested they should: but inside I begged them to break through my role-playing, to sit down beside me and weep with me.

Matthew was quiet as he escorted me to the ward. When faced with a number of possible outcomes to any problem he never speculates. 'If it's this, then that will happen . . .' He waits until it has happened. Thus he did not comment on anything, but he kept me going with his quiet sympathy and love. He was well practised at the whole ritual of my illness, hospitalisation and surgery. He had seen me through it five times before.

They were kind enough to me on the ward, though I felt impatient at being subjected to unnecessary questionings. Partly, I was bored at recounting the history of my illness and partly I longed to escape from the intensity of physical suffering. Having to repeat it gave me less time alone to compose myself and – I suppose – to pray.

'You don't need to ask me that. It's all in my notes," I sighed to a junior nurse at last. She slipped out of my room, biting her lip. Poor girl. A Sister was probably a daunting enough prospect for her to nurse, without my putting her in her place like that.

Once I had been prepared for theatre, I valued my short time alone before 7.00 p.m. I wasn't praying in a formal way; just thinking in front of God. I knew He was with me, though now, as so often, I couldn't feel Him. I kept placing myself in His hands, asking Him to help me to accept how I was. So much putting on of a brave face in front of others had made it difficult for me to understand exactly how I was, even within myself.

Very soon, it seemed, I was being aroused from the anaesthetic. I recognised the sensations from previous operations: the thud as I was lifted from the trolley and dumped back in bed, the inability to cough without pain piercing through me; the helplessness.

I suddenly became aware of someone beside me.

'Can you hear me, Jane?' It was Richard's voice. I grunted, flickered my eyes but they were too heavy to stay open. 'How do you feel?' He was very kind.

'Fine, thanks.' I croaked my usual evasive reply – he would know how I felt; there was no need for me to launch into a moan.

'Well, I – er – thought I'd pop down to see you, to tell you about it.'

'What did you find?' Such a long sentence required me to take a big breath at the end, and I regretted it. Big breaths were very painful.

'It – er – it wasn't too good, actually.' He sounded quite tense. 'Sometimes with an acute infection you get fluid accumulating in the Fallopian tubes; and sometimes there's a little pus. But – er – you had frank pus. And it wasn't neatly contained in your tube. It was all over your pelvis.'

I swallowed. This meant that I had acute peritonitis. There was a pause.

'I knew you'd find it hard to believe so I tried to take a photo.' He knew my hang-ups all right. 'Unfortunately the camera wouldn't work: it was broken! You'll just have to take my word for it.'

The impact of his words hadn't sunk in yet.

'I'm giving you constant intravenous antibiotics for five days.' I knew that putting them directly into my bloodstream was a much more rigorous way of dealing with the infection than giving me pills which I'd been taking since Wednesday.

For the first time I began to realise that Richard was treating this very seriously. He was still hovering beside me. He was very quiet, uneasy, solemn. I rarely saw him like this: only occasionally when he was grieved at seeing a young patient with cancer. He loathed being unable to cure people.

'I think I'd better phone Matthew to tell him.' He sounded a bit happier now that he'd thought of something positive to do. He paused. 'You both know that he can come in and see you any time.'

This final comment before he walked slowly away to the telephone, was the one which made me sense a little of the seriousness of my condition. In those days, to be allowed to visit someone in hospital at any time was a privilege reserved for relatives of people who were really ill – not for those just recovering from operations, and certainly not for the frauds. I was really slow in allowing the facts to percolate through to me, but at last it began to dawn on me that I really was very ill.

The trouble was that so strong was my fear of being labelled a 'sissy' that I fought against and denied my feelings that I was in pain, in order to put on a brave face. I told myself that, however rotten I felt, I must not trust feelings. I pushed to the back of my mind any question that I could in fact be in pain, so effectively that I took a long time to believe it. Richard and, later, Matthew had to repeat over and over to me how I actually was before I could believe that complaining of pain does not necessarily mean I am unacceptable.

And once I did begin to believe it, I actually became really excited. It was strange to be so elated psychologically when, physically, I was very low. But it seemed a wonderful release to know that others did not think I had been moaning and moping about nothing. I felt a certain amount of glee and, I suppose, pride, that I had achieved one aim in life – that of being brave, of keeping my chin up.

Matthew's visit gave me even more reason to feel vindicated. I was lying very still in the bed when he came, and I was passive for a change. I hardly opened my eyes, nor spoke. He stroked my hand gently.

'Richard phoned me last night, you know,' he said steadily.

I nodded. 'He said he was going to.'

'He said, he didn't know how you managed to climb the stairs and walk into the department yesterday when you went to see him.' I smiled. 'He was bewildered. He said, "If it had been you or me, Matthew, we'd only have got there by being carried in on a stretcher!" '

My chest glowed inside me. Perhaps I felt just as I used to many years before when I had proved to my brothers that I could do brave or precarious things like climbing the pear tree to the very top.

Matthew continued, 'He also told me of his resolve never again to believe your face when you're unwell.'

I smiled again, appreciating being understood.

When I opened my eyes I saw his face furrowed as he spoke again. 'I'm glad he seems to have you sussed at last. But . . .' and he held my hand more tightly. He was troubled. 'My dear Jane. He's obviously concerned about you. He said you're seriously ill.' His voice trailed away.

I was quiet for a bit. 'I know,' was all I could say.

Time was measured according to the constant drip, drip of my intravenous infusion. Even this high dose of two different antibiotics did not bring the dramatic improvement which everybody had expected. When the course had finished I still remained far from well. The February days stretched into a week, and even a month. March turned to April.

Easter approached and I was still lying in the same bed in hospital. I may have looked the same; but of course all the time I was becoming weaker.

I became increasingly passive. I had to be encouraged and helped to sit up, because I had little enthusiasm left to get out of bed and prove that I was trying hard to make progress. I had to be cajoled into eating food. The nurses had to pour my drinks and pass them to me in order to maintain my fluid intake. Certainly I could not muster the physical energy to hold a book, never mind concentrate on reading it. I simply looked forward to the brief release brought to me by the pain-killing drugs, although I loathed the side-effects so much that even that respite was tainted by its own dread.

My spirits began to flag. Though never one to give up easily, there was no fight left in me. Two or three times I was allowed home for some days, to see if that would help to raise my morale and bring back my normal huge drive to live. Each time I had to be readmitted within a week or so for pain-killing and anti-sickness injections. Medically, there was very little else that could be done for me: I had been pumped full of drugs, vitamins and even sherry, courtesy of the NHS! Yet I remained pale, listless, uninterested, ill and in pain. Always I was in pain; more pain, I feared, than I would be able to bear.

For one of my spells out of hospital, I stayed in the home of one of Matthew's college lecturers, Tina.

In hospital I had yearned to be nearer to Matthew and I also wanted to be within the deeply caring fellowship of his theological college.

There was a group of people who had joined together to pray every Monday since I had been admitted to hospital in February. They and others had also reached out to me by visiting me, or by writing to me, or by sending thoughtful messages via Matthew. God's love was clearly seen among so many people in college, I wanted to drink in as much of it as possible. The atmosphere was hardly comparable with hospital! With persuasion, Richard had conceded that I could be discharged into Tina's care.

Poor Tina. I do not know if she knew what she was taking on. For me, my time in her home was like an oasis, spiritually, where I could drink in the comfort and love. But in every other way, I sank lower and lower.

Matthew and I, by being nearer to one another, could see more clearly how far from my normal self I was. In Tina's flat, we were both confronted by the extent to which my pain imposed on the expression of our relationship. We could not enjoy quiet, intimate conversations because there was always the unspoken tension of my illness preventing us from being totally relaxed: and of course any physical expression of relationship was completely thwarted.

I began to wonder if Matthew ever considered how much better off he would have been if he had married someone else. I asked him what he would do if I should die. Every time I asked, he talked of returning to Sarawak where he had once taught. We both knew that he would never be able to fulfil this desire with me, because of my medical history.

The seed of doubt was sown in my mind. Would it not be to Matthew's benefit if I were to die? Of course he would mourn, he would grieve – but would he not ultimately be more free if he were not burdened by me living in pain?

Throughout my sleepless nights I pondered the burden I am on others. My conclusion was always the same. However hard I had tried to make the gift of my life outweigh the burden of it, I was failing. I was certain that I was more burden than gift.

Even apart from Matthew I thought of the burden I was on Tina, on others having to visit me. I could not perceive that they themselves might be gaining anything. I believed that weakness was a waste. I did not recognise any value in my life, either for myself or for them watching me. I was all burden – even to myself. I had struggled on for so long, eventually I became weary and sick of life itself. Finally one day, I gave up hope.

It happened because of a telephone call to the hospital seeking help. I had to tell Richard I was unable to tolerate the dreadful pain any longer.

I was unable to speak to Richard himself, but another Sister, Pat, listened very understandingly. She took my message and promised to phone me back.

The silence in Tina's flat was suddenly broken by Pat's return phone call. I struggled to crawl over and answer it.

'Jane?' Pat spoke very gently.

'Yes, hi.' I put on my normal jovial voice. 'What did Richard say?'

'He said, keep going.'

'But Pat, I phoned because I've run out of resources to be able to.'

'Well, he said that when or if things get back to being as bad as they were in February then you must come back to him.'

I wondered how I could explain myself more clearly. 'Things *are* back to being as they were in February. In fact I feel worse. I've no strength left with which to fight now.'

'You're that bad, Jane?' Pat wanted to be sure she had the message right. 'Remember how seriously ill you were then.'

I remembered all right. 'Pat, I'm desperate. I can't go on.'

'Hang on. I'll phone you back again.'

I knew that each time she went, she must be interrupting Richard in between patients at his busy Wednesday morning clinic. Normally, I would have been helping him. I knew he hated interruptions. She must have been doing her diplomatic act.

I knelt on the floor of Tina's hallway, leaning over the low table whilst I waited the second time. I could not face the tedium of making my way clumsily to a comfortable chair. No chair was comfortable in any case – no chair, nor bed, nor any position. I could not escape.

Pat did not take long. This time her voice, though still gentle, was strained. 'I've spoken again to Richard and explained better how you are.' She hesitated. 'He said that you must be assured you can come into hospital at any time, day or night, for adequate pain relief.'

I could not believe my ears. I was being given the instructions we give to patients having terminal care. This was what we said to patients when we could not cure them . . .

There was no emotion in my voice when I spoke. 'Was there nothing else he said? Can't he do anything else, Pat?'

Pat was obviously choosing her words carefully. 'He said there is nothing more positive he can do.' Then she added, 'He felt very helpless and very sorry for you.'

I replaced the receiver. So, that was it then. I made my way to the sitting-room. My mind was completely vacant, numb, except for the words, 'Nothing more he can do . . . nothing more he can do.'

I do not recall how many people I stared through as the day progressed. It was as if I had been given an anaesthetic which numbed me completely, though I was not asleep.

One visit I do remember, though. Matthew was with me when Colin, the college principal, came. I thought of him as a shy man with little time for small talk in his busy life, but he had been wonderful throughout my illness, visiting me frequently in hospital. I was very grateful, though I stood enough in awe of him to fear that, were I to share my deepest reactions, he might find them rather trite.

Colin asked me how I felt. My answer was, I had thought, suitably objective. I avoided telling him how I felt emotionally; and chose rather to give him factual information. I told him of my phone call that morning.

Colin sat for a long time, keeping his gaze on me until at last he asked, 'Does this mean death, Jane?'

I was startled.

'Pardon?' I asked, killing time. I was most uncomfortable. I was not used to talking intimately with Colin and he was pretty near the bone now. I was terrified I might cry – courageous me, in front of Colin to whom I did not wish to appear a weepy woman! And what would Matthew think? I was acutely embarrassed that he was there, listening. How did Colin dare to be so direct as this?

He repeated his question. 'Does this mean death?'

I knew he expected an answer from me. I looked at Matthew. With relief I saw he was not surprised by Colin. I tried to follow his example and keep calm.

'I suppose it does . . . yes.'

I will never forget Colin's help, though I cannot recall anything he said. He stayed with us. He counselled us, prayed with us. With his help, Matthew and I had joined hands and faced my death together. And we had not been left alone.

But that afternoon, something snapped. Thoughts of my death became urgent. Suddenly I felt unable to wait any longer. I could not go through with any more.

This was my Gethsemane. The pain was too much. God was asking too much. I had that huge bottle of pills which Richard had prescribed in February with his 'joke' about not taking them all at once. Wouldn't it help me, and Matthew, and Tina and Colin and all those in college, if I just speeded things up? Wouldn't that give a nice happy ending instead of my having to bear this seemingly endless pain?

In the middle of the night the temptation became

unbearable.

'Tina!' I cried out, at the top of my voice.

And to God I cried in a whisper, 'Let this cup pass from me . . .'

2

'Not as I will, but as you will'

(Matthew 26:39b)

If Tina had preached to me about the goodness of
God, I would never have come through as I did.
The fact was, God seemed not to care a toss that I
was at the end of my tether. Yet even in the depths
of my anguish, there was in me some stirring of
affirmation that I wanted what God wanted, and
that I must not take my own way out.

'I mustn't, must I?' I whispered, clutching the
bottle of pills.

Tina's curlers clung resolutely to the ends of her
hair. Her ample bosom heaved rather breathlessly
as her eyes focused to take in the scene: a bucket
beside my bed, lest an overdose should have made
me vomit; a towel laid neatly across the sheet lest
I should have made a mess; the desperation which
must have registered on my face.

Quickly she moved forward to kneel beside the
bed, taking both my hands in hers. 'Have you
taken any?' Her voice was earnest; she had realised
immediately the implications of what she saw.

I shook my head.

I could not speak now. Words seemed trite, inadequate; too shallow to describe the depths I felt. It was as if my experience of suffering had led me to see through a window beyond which there lay a whole world. The world on which I was gazing that night was the mystery of suffering.

As Tina knelt beside me, the silent bond between us began to infuse warmth into my numbness against life. If I felt nothing else, I was at least glad I was not alone whilst my eyes were opened to see that huge mysterious world. I suspect that she, too, saw the same picture as I.

Eventually I spoke. 'God is asking too much of me.'

The last thing I wanted was theology or anything – anything – other than loving understanding. I needed to hear that yes, this really was unbearable, and indeed that the worst, most devastating aspect was that God was not rescuing me from intolerable pain.

The compassion in Tina's eyes did not fade. With relief, I realised that she was not judging me. It was as if she knew that we were both looking towards the infinite, the unanswerable. To have imagined we could give an answer with our finite minds, would have been to deny what we were seeing.

With Tina's ability to hold my anguish without denying it or explaining it away, came the softness of tears. They began to flow down the cheeks of us both: tears of agony but also of relief that I was not being rejected even when hurling such strong questions into the air.

'How can He allow this pain to go on so

long? How can I express to Him that this is too much . . . ?' I was crying aloud now.

Slowly, very gently, Tina began to speak. Her voice was very soft, almost a whisper. 'I don't know,' she said when my sobbing began to ease. She knew I was not really asking her; I was shouting at God! I was trying to demand that He explain Himself to me.

She must have known that she would have squashed me if she had sounded strong in the face of my weakness. She must have been aware that we were both at the mercy of God and where He would lead us. She showed no pride that she had not been tempted as I had been only minutes before. She knew that she could have been led to the same place as me, had God so allowed.

'I don't understand Him,' she said softly. 'He does seem to ask an awful lot of some people sometimes.' She looked at her hands and her voice trailed away. She had obviously reminded herself of a time when God had seemed harsh to her.

There was a silence between us. I could see that it was hard for Tina to struggle with the memory of her pain. But her gentleness with me showed she had reached the point of acceptance: even though that point has to be reached again and again each time one relives the pain in one's mind. In these moments of loving sympathy Tina, almost unwittingly, was leading me towards a most important and health-giving insight. I – a fighter by nature – began to see that God wanted to give me the strength not to fight against His will, but to embrace it. I thus began to understand one of the key 'secrets' within the mystery of suffering.

I lay back against the pillows for the first time

that night. Slowly the tension I had felt began to ease just a little as Tina's compassion shone through her words. As her story was gradually unfolded, I realised that she was not surprised by my being at the end of my tether. She had been in that place herself. It was good for me to be taken into the heart of someone else's suffering. This was true compassion: 'with suffering'. She was able to share the burden of my pain because she recognised it. Because she had refused to run away from the hard questions within herself, she could also face them in me.

It was not her story which was so moving, but the manner in which she talked. Her quietness and calmness spoke, more clearly than any words, of her complete acceptance of me in my despair. She was offering me the same acceptance which she had found for herself. She knew she would never completely understand God's wisdom. She had therefore allowed some questions to remain. She accepted the mystery of suffering.

The more I listened, the more encouraged I felt. Not that I was pleased that she had suffered so much; nor was there any special comfort in knowing that I was not the only person ever to experience Gethsemane. The source of my encouragement was the realisation that I was not being dreadfully unchristian for feeling as I did. If Tina had been taken to similar depths and desperation (and her story caused me to admire her all the more for it), then maybe I should not condemn myself.

I suddenly realised that probably many people have suffered similarly, but that they have not dared to talk about it for fear that an intimately personal experience should be explained glibly away by someone who could not understand.

Before leaving me to rest for the last few hours of the night, Tina prayed with me. She did not impose any pious-sounding prayers. She spoke slowly, even haltingly, for she respected the very personal area between me and God where she knew she was treading.

In quietness and stillness she sought God's will with me. She asked that if, as it seemed, God was not going to rescue me *from* the suffering, I might know Him *in* it. Her prayer could not have been more appropriate. This was one of the times in life when to struggle to escape suffering was to lose touch with God. To accept it was to find His presence; that loving presence who never leaves us nor forsakes us even in the harsh reality of pain.

The following day dawned bright and sunny. Everything seemed to have a heightened significance; every aspect of the world going round drew my attention. The sky was clear and blue, the spring air fresh. While I waited for Matthew to call in on his way to morning worship, I was intrigued to watch the birds in the trees outside. They were not fighting their way through life. They just got on with it, busily content with everyday things. They chirped and sang; they flitted across to a different branch for a change of scene; they looked for worms on the lawn; they flew high and swooped down again. They were carefree. They were not questioning how long they would live. When difficulties arose they would either overcome them or they would die. They were not overburdened about that.

Perhaps, I thought, I should learn from the birds.

My musings were interrupted by the welcome click of the door. The moment Matthew entered I clung to him fervently. In holding him as I did, I think I was acknowledging a deeply subconscious intent to hold on to life in this world.

Gradually I dared to give him hints as to what had happened during the night. The more he understood, the more he enabled me to unfold the full story of my temptation. He skipped his first lecture in order to prolong our blessed time, together for a while, silently affirming our allegiance to one another. The comfort I felt from him – and later from others – was a lifeline. How much I needed the love and absence of condemnation they expressed to me! Now I no longer felt so alone.

The reassurance and acceptance I received brought comfort. And comfort brought courage: the courage to be weak. Strengthened by that, I experienced some sort of breakthrough. From this time onwards I began to grow deeper and deeper into an acceptance of God's will for me, however hard it was to be.

I was still critically ill. Other people noticed and remarked upon the deep-down spirit of peace which welled up from within me. As my week in Tina's home drew to an end, the college closed for Easter. I very much wanted to go to the final Thursday evening communion. I knew it might be my last. I wanted to be in college among so very many caring Christians who had supported me in prayer through the long months.

It was a struggle to go the few yards from Tina's college flat to the chapel, but I wanted to make the effort. I remember Caroline helping to dress me, as I felt too weak for even that exertion. Once outside,

I leaned my weak body against a supportive arm. Almost every step was an act of will.

'Just get yourself to that handrail. Walk! Keep going!'

'Rest your weight on that door-handle for a minute, then walk again. Get to the next door before stopping again. Force yourself! Don't lose your momentum.'

I recall one door being opened for me by someone who had heard how ill I was but who had not seen me since February. As I walked through the door, his face suddenly froze. I still chuckle to myself as I picture him literally jumping to attention with a click of his heels. He almost saluted. If he had not been quite so frightened by his close proximity to death (in my person) I would have spoken the words in my head, 'Don't worry, I'm not in my coffin yet!'

The chapel doors were open when I approached and I could hear the welcoming hum of conversation before the service began. It was two months since I had been part of a service, and my spirits rose excitedly. Although it was only forty-eight hours since that terrible night with Tina, now as I neared the chapel I knew for myself that I had been given a new peace which others had seen in me. Assuredly, this peace passes all human understanding – for, humanly speaking, nothing had changed. I had no reason to be peaceful, no hope of cure or of the release of death being any nearer, no magic pills to relieve the pain and nausea. Yet I was filled right up to the top with God's peace.

I was handed my hymn-book by a student named John. My heart and soul began to be filled even more with God's peace: so much that there was also a joyfulness, and the radiance of this joy merged into an enormous love towards everyone. This can only have been a heavenly gift. It was as if I was darting from one corner of my heart to another, discovering new and wonderful presents from my Lord at every turn.

John was the first person whom I saw as I became aware of what the Lord had given me. As I took the book from his outstretched hand, I could see he was looking at me closely. I beamed at him and even then I remember thinking that the broadest of smiles could not reflect the joy within me.

Years later, I learned that John ran home after that chapel service and told his wife excitedly, 'I've seen Jane Grayshon! I've seen her face! I didn't know who she was before but I recognised her immediately. She was stooping physically – but her face! It glowed. She was absolutely radiant. I couldn't stop watching her radiance all through the service.' And he was inspired to write a beautiful poem.

This joy, which had emerged from the deep peace, was the joy from accepting God's way for me. I had reached the point of conceding even subconsciously, 'Not as I will, but as you will, o Lord.'

This was not a passive submission to what I could not change. I had not resigned myself to God's will. I had done something much more positive than that. I had begun to embrace God's will, and as a result I discovered that some precious fruit was growing even within my suffering. Indeed, it grew from the very root of acceptance which Tina had offered to me.

* * *

The following two months were a hard test of this acceptance. Nothing changed dramatically. It was as if the whole scenario was held still; as if God was holding the whole situation before me and asking, 'Will you still accept My will, Jane? Or are you merely accepting My will because you hope that will bring about a change in the situation? For how long will you endure for My sake? As long as I desire, or until you run out of patience?'

But my trust in my Lord did not flag again. Indeed, as the weeks of April and May passed, so my acceptance of His will grew.

During this lull in the storm, while I became no better, but no worse either, someone from the prayer group heard me comment that only the sunshine in the Bahamas would do me any good. A seed was sown in her mind.

There were about ten couples who had committed themselves to prayer each week, all students on meagre grants. Yet their desire was to be open to what God wanted. They were willing to do anything practical to help Matthew and myself – not 'just' to pray.

Within a week of my comment, I was presented with an envelope. I could see that it was a card – another one among ninety or so, all assuring me that friends cared about me and were thinking of me. I laid this one on the table beside my bed. I would enjoy Caroline's visit now and could look forward to opening it later after she had gone.

'Aren't you going to open it then?' Caroline's voice almost sounded hurt, but her eyes sparkled with excitement.

'Oh . . . all right then,' I conceded. Wearily, I slit along the white envelope and pulled out the card.

Something slipped out from between the folds on to my blankets, followed by a £10 note. I handled the money and then picked up the other paper from between the folds. It was a cheque. I turned it over to read it: 'Four hundred and ten pounds only'.

I looked at the words incredulously. Caroline was almost dancing on the bed. She knew the wonderful freedom and pleasure of giving in response to God. She, and the whole group, had not held fund-raising events. They had prayed to God to help me; they had listened to Him; and now they responded by giving whatever they felt right. They had managed to double a gift Matthew's mother had lovingly promised to us.

'You can have your holiday in the sun!' said Caroline, impatient with my stunned silence. Her voice was almost squeaking, such was her joy in giving.

I had only just begun to believe what we had been given, when Colin dropped by once again. About twice each day he showed his continuing care and support.

I handed him the envelope.

He was kneeling on the floor beside the bed, just as Tina had done only three nights before. Now it was his turn to be silenced. His eyes moistened as he witnessed such love and involvement of Christian friends.

When others heard of the cheque they too joined in with their prayerful contributions until we could have a really big holiday. 'If all you can do is lie down, then go and do that – but in the sun,' they said.

So we did. After browsing through brochures, we took off. We had chosen a tiny island fifty miles from Madeira, with only one hotel and a long white beach. This was my longest spell out of hospital. We felt free – free from hospital routines, visiting hours, telephone calls from caring relations. For almost two weeks we were together, alone.

Matthew's biggest problem now was stopping me from swimming! My natural love of water and sport, combined with the lure of the balmy turquoise water, almost overcame common sense. I lacked the physical strength to swim safely so I had to be content with quick dips to cool off from the sun. Instead, I developed a beautiful sun-tan.

Unfortunately my honey-coloured skin which made me look so well was misleading. My temporary respite was not to last long.

I accompanied Matthew to college in May. Our welcome back was wonderful. For some people it was like seeing me return from the dead – the last time they had seen me was at the communion service before the Easter holiday, when I had been pale and drawn.

'Jane – you look so much better! You look wonderful.'

Some people were more misled. 'You *are* so much better,' they said. Perhaps neither they nor I realised how much my colour, heightened by the sun, belied the condition of my inside. 'You *still* look radiant, Jane. How are you?' That sort of comment came from those who took slightly more time to enquire how I felt, rather than presume that my appearance represented how I felt.

Those who knew that I enjoyed a good leg-pull grinned. 'Trust you to wear a white blouse just to accentuate your tan!' I twinkled in reply. Yes, I had to admit I did enjoy being the envy of so many people!

I was wearing a white blouse again not many days later when our latent hopes for a gradual convalescence suddenly plummeted.

It was during another Thursday evening communion service in the college chapel that I realised the abdominal pain was much worse. When pain is severe, it is often hard to say that it is slightly better or slightly worse: pain is always bad! But this Thursday evening there was no doubt that it was growing very much worse.

I resisted my first temptation to whisper to Matthew. I did not think that I could get out of chapel, if he suggested that we leave. Instead, I held on to a hope that it was a spasm which would pass. I heard nothing of the service. My thoughts were entirely taken up with plans as to how I could get out of chapel without drawing attention to myself.

The door was not too far away. But panic rose in me as I glanced towards it and saw the row filled with people whom I would need to pass on my way out. They were all men, too. 'They're sure to think I am a sissy for going out,' I speculated. 'So I can't go.'

Graham, Matthew's tutor who had remained so close to us throughout my illness, was just on Matthew's right. I knew that I would be unable to walk upright. 'I'm supposed to be better. Graham might suppose I'm trying to attract attention to myself, if I walk out bent double now.' I was paralysed by the old fear of being thought a fraud. Graham had been so very caring towards us, I did not want to lose his support by giving him the opportunity to suspect that I was simply exaggerating my symptoms.

This time, though, the physical pain became more acute than my fears. Waiting for it to pass did not work. It got worse until I reached a level of pain which I had not previously known to exist.

A hymn began. I prodded Matthew.

'Can't get up,' I garbled. Once again, every word cost me extra breath; every breath meant more pain searing through me.

'Well, just sit through the hymn, silly,' Matthew replied vaguely without looking at me.

I am normally very pleased when Matthew can enjoy times of release from being weighed down by the solemnity of my suffering. However there was no doubt that on this occasion I had to shatter his freedom and make him realise what I meant.

I slipped my hand into his, ready to try to explain. Matthew was shocked to feel the cold clamminess of my hand. It was wet and slippery with perspiration. He took my hand and then looked at me, questioningly. 'Oh, my dear Jane!' he whispered, seeing my face for the first time. I wondered what my face looked like, for it certainly precipitated an immediate reaction from him!

The piano introduction was over and everyone else stood up to sing. I was thankful for the element of privacy which that brought, for now I could only be seen by one row of people between me and the door.

'Come on.' Matthew left no room for discussion as to whether or not I should leave the service.

'Can't get up.'

I began to be distressed by my helplessness.

Matthew almost lifted me and continued to take much of my weight very discreetly as he accompanied me towards the vestry door. Most of the men were immersed in their singing but as I passed Graham I was again tormented by the fear of being so weak as to be unacceptable. So despite the terrible pain, despite my need to concentrate on every move towards the door, somehow I mustered a big smile for him. It was such a bluff, aimed at preventing him from having any suspicion of what was going on.

The effect of that smile was two-fold. First, it protected me in my embarrassment at being so vulnerable. I did not know how to cope with being visibly outfaced by pain. But while I was successful in avoiding 'making a fuss', I was also cutting Graham off from the opportunity to care or help. It was a high price for me to pay: what I wanted most was – and is – for people to show they care. They cannot cure the pain, but they can comfort me within it. And, like it or not, I needed help.

Once the chapel door was shut behind me, Matthew looked for a chair. There was none there.

'What shall we do?' he asked.

'Must tell Richard.' He was the only one who could really do anything to help. I knew something had happened inside me about which he must be told. Even though it was evening time, there was no doubt that he must see me immediately.

I leaned forwards over the table with my arms

outstretched, and I laid my head on my hands. This felt the only thing I could do to find any relief at all; yet I knew I could not stay there. I raised myself again, catching sight of the reflection of myself in the wall mirror as I did so. With some horror I saw that my sun-tan had disappeared and been replaced by ashen white.

I had to move on. Leaning heavily on Matthew, I staggered to the staircase. For the first time I could sit down, on one of the steps.

'What do you want me to do?' Matthew repeated; but this time he realised that I was beyond being able to think rationally as he could.

'Can't move,' was all I could say in a staccato voice. I nearly panicked at finding myself so helpless, so paralysed by pain. 'I simply can't.'

And yet, strange as it may seem, amidst all this trauma, I was still aware of a deep peace and acceptance undergirding me.

I sat rigid on the step.

Matthew gave me an ultimatum. 'You either let me phone Richard, or the GP, or I get an ambulance,' he stated.

I couldn't have an ambulance coming for me whilst I was conscious! Matthew's ultimatum caused me to muster all my strength again. Slowly, carefully, I pulled myself up and managed to descend a few stairs. Matthew did not press me for an answer – though he must have wondered what on earth would happen next. He swallowed all his own questions in order to keep at my pace in the whole saga, patiently being at my side.

By the time I had reached the bottom of the stairs I had agreed to one of his suggestions. We would

seek help from the caring home of the College
Principal and his wife, Di.

I could trust Di. She would not think of judging
me; she would simply care. As our short spurts
of progress brought us towards Di's house, I had
some carrot of hope for help.

Di did not disappoint us. Her welcome gave us
no indication that she and her daughters had been
in the middle of eating when we rang the bell.
It was almost as if she had been expecting us.
'Jane!' She held her arm out to me in a quiet,
helping gesture. 'You're coming in to lie down?'
She looked to Matthew for confirmation.

Hands helped me to a comfortable chair. The
kind smiles and caring eyes of everyone merged
into a spinning haze of pain. I began to shiver and
shake uncontrollably. Blankets were fetched and
wrapped around me.

'What a granny I must look like,' was the only
thought which penetrated my daze. Then Di was
sponging my face and neck with soothing warm
water, my hands were submerged and the water
was gently swished over them. Allowing them to
float eased away some of the shock. The water
itself was a therapy; the tender care with which
it was done was even more so.

From behind my closed eyes I heard Matthew
telephoning in the hall. He was having difficulty
getting help. The GP was refusing to leave her
clinic to come. Richard was on the golf course and,
though his wife had offered to send a message to
him, it would be some time before he could do
anything.

Matthew returned. He and Di discussed plans.
Di ran off to get another doctor, Cathy, whom

they knew was in the chapel. Immediate help was needed until Richard could be contacted.

Cathy, though whisked out from the chapel service, was unflustered. She did not persist unnecessarily with her examination of me. She soon assessed what injection I needed, and drove off promptly to fetch some.

The morphine had begun to work by the time Colin returned home. He had not seen the various exits from the chapel service earlier, nor knew the story behind them. He leapt two at a time up the steps into his house as usual, and paced straight into the room.

He soon switched his quick mind. 'You not feeling so good, Jane?' He perched himself on a chair. He would always have time to listen when there was a real need.

'Not wonderful,' was my reply. 'Silly, isn't it?' and I tried to chuckle lightly, deflecting from the heaviness which I felt.

Someone else filled in details of the hunt for medical assistance, while my mind drifted in a morphine blur. Colin took it all in. He stayed with us for the remainder of the evening, suspending whatever else he had planned to do. Both Matthew and I noticed appreciatively the sacrifice of his time – most especially because we knew how immensely busy he is. Yet he stopped for those precious hours, simply to be with us.

He was not even 'helping' us formally by counselling us. It might even have looked as if he was ignoring me. When visitors dropped in to see me on their way home from college, Colin thoughtfully steered the conversation away from me. In a mute expression of care he accepted me as I was. He

surely recognised that all I could do was to lie
limply on the sofa and allow any conversation to
drift over me.

Soon the visitors left, the girls retired upstairs
and only Colin and Di sat on with Matthew and
me until the late May twilight.

Tension mounted as the minutes ticked by and
still we waited for at least a message from Richard.
If we did not hear soon, the effect of the injection
would diminish and my state of shock might worsen
seriously. Cathy had insisted she would return
within two hours to attend me if I was still not
in hospital, but I loathed troubling her. I felt I
was a thorough nuisance and wished I could pull
myself together.

Our speculations were stalled by a visit from
Graham. He had only just heard where I was
and why.

'Why on earth didn't you get Matthew to fetch
me out of chapel?' he asked, half chuckling at my
refusal ever to give in, half hurt (I suspect) that
I had seemed not to trust him. 'We could have
carried you down the stairs together.'

I curled up at the notion. 'Please, don't be hurt,'
I pleaded. It was not he who was not trustworthy,
but *I* who did not dare to trust anyone lest I be
thought a fraud.

Like Colin, Graham suppressed any thoughts
for himself. As always, he discerned the most
important issue.

'Are you afraid, Jane?'

I paused before answering. His questions were
always worth thinking about.

'I'm so completely taken up in coping with the
present, I'm not looking ahead.' With the help of

the morphine my sentences could be less brief, my words less staccato.

'But now that I'm asking you?' he pursued. My thoughts raced on to what would be decided about me during the coming night, inevitably in hospital.

'I suppose I am . . . But I'm all right.'

Graham knew of my experience of deep inner peace, arising out of my acceptance that even this pain might be under God's hand. He dared to dig deeper. 'What do you fear most of all?'

I let my mind consider for a moment the various possibilities which lay ahead for me; I wondered what I feared the most among them . . . Certainly it was not the possibility of dying which made me fearful: that would have brought so much relief from the pain that it was a welcome idea. That was the clue to my worst fear.

'Continuation of pain with no prospect of relief,' I said, numbly. 'As you know, I fear another anaesthetic, especially with the memory of not being fully asleep last year before they started doing things to me.'

I shuddered as I remembered the tubes being put down my throat, my body being handled as if I were not conscious, and the horror of being unable to move or show any sign that I was still awake.

'And I fear the weakness and the long, long uphill struggle of recovering from a big operation. But those would be just about bearable if they were successful and worthwhile.' I paused to think about the meaningful type of pain, such as labour pain which, though intense and dreadful at the time, is normally forgotten as soon as it brings forth its purpose – a healthy baby. But this was in stark contrast to my suffering.

'It's the thought of pain with no end, no purpose, no fruit, which is so difficult.' Even as I said it I knew that Graham was helping me by pushing me so far. To stay afraid to examine my inner fears was to allow them scope for destruction: to bring them out into the open was to bring them to the light of God.

Graham understood.

'God doesn't make any mistakes, Jane.' How often he had reinforced that truth to me.

I shook my head. 'I don't feel this is His mistake.' Talking was giving me more confidence in God's will.

Graham smiled. 'How are you so sure of that?'

'Because God is in it.' I myself was amazed to find that that deep-down tranquillity which I had first experienced back in April, had spread from my soul to my mind. Even this immense pain did not quench it. 'It's accompanied by such peace, such an assurance of Him with me that I know it's not His mistake.' Whatever was to follow that night, I knew I was in God's hands. 'I just wish I could get comfortable now.'

And Graham, in his wisdom, could accept what I was expressing. There is a difference between accepting God's will even when He does not promise to give us a comfortable life, and the hard grind of enduring suffering when it comes.

Alone again with Colin and Di, there was a quietness in the room, although the warm homeliness was marred. The increasing urgency with which we awaited the telephone's ring pressed in upon us. Outside, darkness was falling quickly now and there was a chill in the air. Di tucked the blankets around me again and lit the small lamps on the shelf. As she bent down, soft shadows were cast across her cheeks. It was then that I noticed the anxiety in her face.

Suddenly everyone was jerked away from apprehensive speculation. For an uncertain moment, Matthew looked quickly to his host, then he leapt across to answer the shrill telephone himself.

However long the hours of waiting had been, however many times I had rehearsed Richard's reaction in my mind, I was still surprised to hear the stark reality of the words.

Matthew was leaning round the door, relaying instructions. 'We've to meet Richard at the hospital in fifteen minutes. Will you manage to go in our car, or should he send an ambulance?'

'Oh, car, please.' At least Matthew would be sensitive to drive gently and avoid pot-holes in the road. 'Do I really have to go, though?'

Matthew smiled, withdrew back to the phone and let the door close behind him. Colin rose to find my coat; Di came towards me to help me to get up from the sofa. I gathered that I had asked a silly question which warranted no reply.

Somehow, I managed to stand up, but however much I tried I could not straighten myself completely. I felt humiliated to be so stooped and bent. I imagined that if only I could make enough effort, I would succeed in looking normal. I had no idea that I was the only one who expected the impossible of myself.

Inch by inch I staggered across the room, wondering at each step how I could cross the few feet to the door. Colin's face was very compassionate. He opened the door for me, allowing me to see the slight ramp I had to negotiate to get into the car. At that moment I almost felt too daunted. My dismay must have registered on my face.

'Would it not be best if we lifted you?' Colin asked. He must have felt impotent, unable to help me further.

'I shook my head. 'I'm OK,' I muttered. I swallowed hard and gripped the low garden wall. Matthew hovered beside me, encouraging me but still allowing me to feel independent.

Once again the challenge was on. I had to reach the top of the ramp, just as much as I had had to reach the top of the pear tree. To give in would have been to fail in what I thought I was expected to 'achieve'. Thus I willed myself determinedly to get to the car. '. . . Shuffle one foot forward. You must do it. Take a breath. Now the other foot. Don't crack now . . .'

Matthew closed the car door and started the engine. Colin and Di were silhouetted in their doorway against the glowing lights of their warm home. Then as the car turned, the headlights swished round to illuminate their faces. They smiled and waved. Their hearts were with us.

I clenched my hands as the car moved forwards at last. Still the two figures remained on the threshold, gazing out into the night. They waited and watched after us until we were right out of sight. Even when we could no longer see them, we knew that in spirit they were with us, driving into the darkness.

Their lingering presence was a significant sign of what I was slow to appreciate: that while I suffered, they suffered with me.

3

'If one suffers, all suffer'

(1 Corinthians 12:26)

It was hard for Matthew to turn from my bedside and leave the hospital. Driving homewards down the familiar roads his mind was full of the distressing scenes of the evening.

Not that he didn't welcome the respite of a little time to himself back home. It was already well past midnight and he, too, was exhausted. The difficulty was in walking away from such anguish. He might have seemed to be turning his back on me, betraying me in my hour of need. And yet, he reasoned with himself, was this night any different? For so many months we had endured living on a knife-edge, hovering between serious illness and critical. It had all gone on for so long that it had gradually become a part of both our lives.

Matthew was no longer living alongside me with my pain: he was living in his own pain. The pain of watching, of waiting and weeping is equally as lonely as any physical hurt.

Uppermost in his mind as he drove home now

was the vision of Richard's face, solemn and unmoving. What had been in his mind? Was there more he might do to help? Was there further treatment to which he could resort?

Richard had shown no sign of emotion. He had gone through everything in a businesslike manner. Perhaps he, too, felt a measure of distress but could not show it lest that should affect his clinical judgement. I was the patient, he the helper. He would surely be failing if he became a victim to suffering as well.

'I'm very sorry,' he had said numbly. 'Just to complicate matters, I'm afraid that tomorrow I'm off to France for the weekend.' His eyes fixed thoughtfully on the shiny hospital floor.

A weekend? That seemed an unbearably long time! I would surely not be able to cling to life until Monday?

Fear must have registered in my eyes and Richard must have reached the same conclusion. 'I must get the Professor's opinion,' he had announced, walking purposefully to the telephone.

Suddenly, things began to move. After weeks and months of not knowing what to do, the medical profession seemed galvanised into action. I was transferred temporarily to the care of the Professor. On the following day, another surgeon was brought in to give his opinion. Richard was telephoning from France to hear what was happening.

The problem was whether or not they should operate. They hesitated to do so: I might not have survived the anaesthetic. But the Professor's reluctance was for a different reason. He was increasingly insistent that they could not be certain what exactly more surgery would hope to achieve.

Once again I was pumped full of injections – a constant infusion of antibiotics, vitamins, nourishment. Once again, whenever Matthew saw me I was lying pale, listless and exhausted by pain.

Then one day things came to a head at a case conference in the ward. The dynamics had become strained. Richard, back from his holiday weekend, was technically back to being in overall charge of me, but he was nevertheless junior to the Professor. He had been surprised that another laparotomy had not been done in his absence: but how could he express this horror to his boss? His judgement was based more on how ill he sensed I was, than on specific medical tests. He was very concerned. In comparison, the Professor seemed intent on appearing relaxed about my condition. He had reinforced that most firmly by strolling into the ward office for the case conference forty minutes late.

By this time, Richard was seething. Perhaps, again, he was subconsciously suffering. He had to endure the feelings of impotence and possibly also of self-doubt that were part of being unable to make me better. He barely raised his eyes to greet the late comer. He had not guessed then that even the Professor could have felt pain from the whole situation – that his difficult attitude might have been a tell-tale sign of his own uneasiness. 'You've resorted to surgical intervention unnecessarily in the past,' came the stinging accusation.

There was a pause. Richard refused to rise to such bait. The Professor flicked through my case notes. 'Look at this histology report. "Normal tissue" you removed last time . . .' He thrust the brown folder into Richard's hands.

The tension rose. Richard hesitated to steady his voice: his very competence was called into question. 'I am telling you,' he said, 'I saw what I removed and I can still see it now. That piece of paper reports what the histology department saw under the microscope. It does not report what was visible to the eye: that the ovary I removed was macroscopically abnormal. It was an obvious cause of severe abdominal pain. As evidence, Jane was much improved for six months post operation, until this acute peritonitis flared up again in February.'

There was little further discussion. From my bed only a short distance away Matthew and I, waiting for them, heard the handle of the office door be turned angrily as the door was flung open.

Only their heavy footsteps punctuated the strained silence between them as they approached my bed. Each man's face appeared firm and hard. Matthew's hand closed more tightly round my thin wrist. He was tense too, waiting to hear of their decision.

Richard had almost been silenced by now; he simply nodded kindly to Matthew. It was the Professor who, accustomed to acting as chairman, gave their report. Involuntarily I drew breath as I listened.

'As you know, Jane has had a lot of problems with peritoneal inflammation.' He was addressing Matthew rather than me. 'She seems to be having continued pain despite our conservative medical treatment on drugs . . .'

'Conservative?' questioned Richard in a whisper, which was nevertheless an interruption. He ran his eyes up and down the length of the intravenous

infusions with the two lots of strong-dose antibiotics. The appropriateness of his query succeeded
in causing irritation in the midst of a rather pompous speech.

'And therefore,' the voice continued more
loudly, 'we have decided that there is no course
of action left to us except further surgery.'

Matthew was uncomfortable at having to receive
this information so passively, especially in this
atmosphere. The only active thing he could do was
to speak, even though that was with a question.

'What do you propose doing?'

My heart beat faster, harder.

The Professor hesitated slightly before meeting
Matthew's uncertain gaze.

'Clear the pelvis.' He cleared his throat, turned
away and walked a few steps to the end of my bed.
He seemed to be distancing himself in every way.

Then straightening up, he faced Matthew again.
From the safety of his familiar role he launched
into a verbose explanation, as if he were lecturing students. When pain threatened to disturb
his equanimity, he retreated into using academic
language.

'A total pelvic clearance . . .' he began. I did not
listen. With my knowledge as a midwife, I needed
no explanation anyway. He had said only what I
had expected. He meant a hysterectomy, but he
could not bring himself to use the word. 'Total
pelvic clearance' sounded more remote.

A host of different emotions welled up inside
me, each one clamouring for my attention. I lay
back on the pillows numbly, allowing the whole
conversation to go over my head.

They could have been discussing someone else,

any old patient. Where was their care and concern? Had it been completely swallowed up in the un-spoken rivalry between the two specialists? I could have been Exhibit A, a subject who was a useful example of what the Professor was explaining. And Matthew could have been a young schoolboy being bombarded with statements.

'You'll have to understand that if we go ahead, this means no children. Removing a uterus means removing all child-bearing potential.'

It was ridiculous. As if we didn't know! And with that choice of words I felt like a cow, a machine; anything but a person. I wanted to shout out, 'Stop it! I have feelings; haven't you?' But maybe it was precisely because he found it so hard that the Professor adopted his unfortunate manner. Maybe it felt safer for him to sound objective, clinical, detached. Maybe to have shown more tenderness would have made him more aware of the suffering my pain caused in him.

The following month or so has become a blur. I have probably blotted things from my mind in my subconscious drive not to dwell on such painful memories. In a sense, this was the end for me; the end of so much . . . so many hopes, so many dreams, so many expectations. Yet it was the beginning of the end of more important things too. The profound illness which had engulfed me for four months since February would always leave its scar, but its terrifying intensity was soon to recede.

Only a few things haunt me, standing out as they do among what, otherwise, my mind refuses to recall. First there was the terrible waiting, waiting for the appointed day of operation. In the climate of his relationship with the Professor, Richard had made a resolve. He would not carry out this operation without the Professor there. He knew how much the Professor's opinion was disadvantaged if he relied solely on histology reports for his clinical judgement. Until he had seen with his own eyes the state of my insides, he was sure the Professor would not believe either me or Richard. Only by this means would Richard's own judgement be vindicated – which he determined to do.

Thus, despite my frail state, both physically and no doubt emotionally, I was caught in the midst of the friction. My operation seemed to serve as an opportunity for the two consultants to engage in a duel.

At last the activity around me increased as the preparations for my operation began. I knew so well the humiliating procedures which, though mundane, heralded surgery which for me would be profound in its lifelong effects.

'You mustn't drink anything now, Mrs Grayshon.' The nurses were busily sticking tubes everywhere – yes, everywhere.

'I'm just going to give you a little enema, Mrs Grayshon.'

Little? I thought.

'I'm just going to put a little tube into your bladder, Mrs Grayshon.' Why did they keep using the word 'little'? To try to make the overall problem seem smaller?

'I'm just going to give you a little shave, Mrs Grayshon.'

Everything they did was all too familiar to me. I'd travelled this way so often before, I could have spoken their words of 'reassurance' myself.

When, finally, the waiting was over, I lay in the anaesthetic room before being put to sleep. Wherever I looked, my eyes seemed to fall upon something which held nightmarish memories for me. The trolley with a ventilator reminded me of when I could not breathe for myself; the clear bottles of drugs seemed to reinforce that this was my seventh operation; the needles seemed poised ready to inflict once again that feeling of vulnerability which I dread with every anaesthetic.

My eyes closed to try to escape the memories. Apprehensively I speculated once again on the outcome of this operation. The form on which I had signed my consent had read: 'Exploratory laparotomy [meaning a jolly good look inside my abdomen] and maybe proceed to total pelvic clearance.' Would things be bad enough for that, I wondered? Or was I slightly better now? Might they find that the infection had resolved and I now had little reason for complaining still of pain?

Richard had already gone through to the theatre. When I had seen him, he was twisting his fingers together nervously. He too was apprehensive. It was his professional expertise which was about to be exposed on the operating table. Would he be vindicated in his boss's eyes? I rubbed the cold sweat from my hands on the skimpy sheet draped over me. I wished this waiting would end.

At that moment the Professor breezed in. I hardly recognised him at first. He was disguised in his theatre garb and I was peering through the haze of my premed injection. Then he spoke in his distinctive accent.

'Ah well,' he chuckled. 'The truth will out now, eh?'

'Pardon?' I was struggling to distinguish his words from behind his flimsy green face-mask.

'I say, the truth will out now!' he repeated. I think he also muttered something about me looking bright-eyed and bushy-tailed. Was he saying I was a fraud?

No sooner had that question raced into my mind than the theatre's swing-door banged closed. He had gone. The anaesthetist had taken my arm now and was already injecting his drug. The black rubber door squeaked open again. Richard popped his head round, only his dark eyes showing between mask and hat. They crinkled with a reassuring smile.

'See you in there,' I heard him say. The buzzing in my ears dragged me into an oppressive sleep.

From a great distance someone was calling me. 'Jane?' My body was too heavy. 'Jane?' My breathing felt laboured. 'Jane?' Oh, I was so weary. 'Can you hear me, Jane?' Yes, I could hear. But I didn't want to hear. I was too tired. She couldn't have realised how badly I needed to sleep. Who was 'she' anyway?

I was standing in a field. I could smell flowers, growing among the corn. They were stale. Every breath I took brought with it the stale smell. It was nauseating. Why was it not sweet? I breathed again.

I tried to turn away from the field of flowers. Whichever way I turned, it stretched ahead of me. I could not get away from it. And the smell once again swept over me. I had to draw another breath. It seemed I was filled with the foul smell. I was very sick.

Something cold and metallic was pushed under my chin. What was this? Perhaps I was not alone. Why could I not see anyone else?

The air was putrid now. If only I could escape the smell. I did not understand, then, that it was my own breath, heavy with the anaesthetic gases, which was inescapable.

'Jane? Can you take a big breath for me?' I wondered why I should want to take a big breath? That would increase the oppressive smell. It was enough to take my little gasps.

The voice altered. 'Better give more oxygen,' it whispered. A mask was pushed over my face. Its plastic aroma mingled with the stale flowers in my field. It made me feel even more trapped.

'You've had your operation, dear.' My operation? Oh. Oh, I see. Yes, that's right. My operation. Well, what had they found then? What had they done?

My questions faded as I drifted back to the field. The next minute (or so it seemed) I was being bumped and battered. I must be being wheeled on a trolley, I realised. Dit-dit. Lift doors were crashed open. Dit-dit. Two more wheels crashed over the threshold into the lift. Whirrrrr. The doors were opened again. Dit-dit. Dit-dit.

'You're back in the ward now, Jane.' It was the friendly Sister speaking. I nodded silently, my eyes still closed. Gradually my field faded, giving way to the slow assimilation of what was happening.

I tried to ask questions. 'What . . . ?' But my mouth would not work properly.

The Sister bent over me. She lacked no imagination as to how I felt. She was the sensitive kind of nurse.

'It's all over, Jane.' Oh, if only that were true, I thought. And what had they actually found? What had they done?

'What . . . ?' was the only word I could muster.

Sister understood. She was a gem. 'They did what they feared they would have to do.' Her discretion never faltered. She knew it was the Professor who ought to tell me; but she also honoured that I was ready to hear now. I had had a hysterectomy.

I nodded again, and drifted back to my field.

It was the Professor's presence which I remember next. He had entered rather more stealthily than his confident approach in the anaesthetic room before theatre. He commented on the operation, repeating to me their findings. Everything has blurred into a smudge of a memory now. Only one of his remarks do I remember. He asked innocently, 'I expect you were in pain beforehand were you, Jane?'

In pain? What could I say? Pain seemed such an underestimation of what I had experienced, such a glib word for such depth of agony. After all, I had felt that I would die.

'I was a little,' I replied distantly. Words could never have formed an adequate answer to him, so I did not try.

I was a little more alert a few days later when Richard came again to discuss things with me. He did not hide his astonishment at my progress as I stood up and twirled around proudly. 'The discomfort from this operation is nothing, compared . . .' I remarked with glee.

'You just be careful,' he warned, but I could see from the gleam in his eye that he was both thrilled and relieved to see my progress.

I had my questions for him, too.

'Which one of you decided?' I asked, intrigued to learn how the dynamics had resolved between the two surgeons.

'Neither of us,' came the cool, measured reply. 'As soon as we'd opened you up, there was no question in either of our minds. The decision lay staring up at us on the table.'

Then Richard's face suddenly twinkled. 'By the way, I got the histology report back today,' he told me. 'It reads, "Normal tissue".'

For a second I was confused. How could it be 'normal' when Richard had only just told me how bad it looked?

'Oh?' I looked up at him questioningly. And suddenly I saw the mischief in his dimple, and I understood. It *was* confusing; I *was* confusing medically. But that did not mean my illness could be denied as some found it easy to suggest.

'I've left it on the Professor's desk for him to find,' he ended. We both smiled, sharing the irony in silence.

Even now nobody had used the word 'hyster-ectomy'. While the phrase 'total pelvic clearance' was accurate, it gave no indication of any loss I may have felt. So I tried not to feel any. I tried to be brave. I joined in the talk about it as if I were strong and courageous like those men. Once again, my childhood years with my brothers served me very well. I had had much practice in suppressing any girlish, sissy-ish wallowing.

Until one evening. A familiar nurse was in charge of the ward. She was new to this ward, though I had once worked with her elsewhere. She must have found it difficult on this evening because our usual roles were reversed. I, more senior to her as a Sister, was now in bed; she was in a position to tell me what to do.

She bounded gaily into the room. She was obviously very pleased with herself. Her harsh, piercing voice grated on my ears. Her words pierced through at me.

'I heard you had your hyst., dear,' she said, smiling broadly.

It was as if the ground had been whisked from under my feet. I did not know what to say, or where to look. It would have hurt me too much to think. Instead, I still recall how enormous was my urge to do something to humiliate her back. She had marched in and trampled all over my feelings. I do not know how I refrained from carrying out the sole idea in my head. I wanted to pick up the jug of cold water from my locker and pour it right over her head.

Everything about that nurse spoke of her care for herself more than for any patient. Her loud, smart shoes demonstrated that she preferred to look good than respect a sick person's need for quietness. Her stark make-up reflected the trouble she took to present an artificial image rather than genuine, self-giving care.

She was relishing the fact that I was vulnerable. She saw that as an opportunity to be a cut above me. I had once told her off for smoking in the loos and she had resented my authority. She had never understood why I asked her to talk more gently to the patients. 'Bit of light-hearted fun never did anyone any harm,' she would retort.

The last thing I wanted that evening was 'a bit of light-hearted fun'. For the first time I was being courageous enough to feel somewhat low. I suppose

I was allowing the first waves of realisation of what a hysterectomy means, to penetrate my heart. Now my loss was being devalued again, even by the abbreviation to 'hyst.'. I felt crushed.

I lacked compassion at the time, but I now realise that the nurse did not know what to say or how to cope with my suffering. She tried to hide under light-hearted words, but her awkward pain was still there. Unfortunately, I just happened to be the one to bear the inappropriateness of her brashness.

Over and over again, my pain caused others to suffer with me . . . Matthew, doctors, nurses. Family and friends who cared for me had their pain, too. They wanted me to be healed. Then all too easily there would be a cycle of hurt, of self-protection, of hiding lest we be hurt further. Occasionally I felt hurt by the silence, not recognising that that concealed others' care. But shortly afterwards, a letter from Geoff seemed to explain it all, and helped me to understand much better:

> Your suffering is painful to many, Jane, and they cannot cope because they love you so much. So, because of the pain they cannot express the depth of love that they are longing to share with you and which you are longing to receive. Accept the love of many, for it exists, and be motivated to live for the sake of all those who cry out but make no sound.

No one suffers in isolation. I had thought that those who make no sound had forsaken me, but Geoff taught me to look beyond what people say – or fail to say.

As the days progressed I began to recover slowly

from the hysterectomy. I could see relief on the faces of those who had suffered through this long trial with me. Everyone was rejoicing. Yet still I was weak, and very much aware of it. Wouldn't it still have been better if things had turned out differently? Was it not true that 'to die is gain'?

Part 2

Living in pain

4

'To live is Christ and to die is gain'

(Philippians 1:21)

As soon as I began to be convalescent, rather than ill, I wanted to embrace life as a gift. The inescapable reality, however, was that for much of the time my body felt like a heavy weight for me to carry around: a burden to my otherwise carefree spirit.

The long uphill struggle towards recovery after an operation is all very vivid to me at this moment. As I write, now six years after my hysterectomy, in 1980, I am again recovering from yet another operation.

Another . . . and another. The word is so simply written: but each time it denotes a particular experience of seemingly unending suffering. In one sense it's as if I have a nightmare which has just repeated itself. Only, I do not dream it. I have to live it.

And therein lies my agony. If it were a nightmare, I would hope to waken up and discover the freedom of the pain's absence. How often that has been my greatest longing! Often I have longed that the pain might go. Often, it has seemed that to die would indeed be gain for me.

Was I being ungrateful for progress? It sounds so. Could I not count my blessings and cheer myself up? Frankly, no. I had experienced God's light in the darkness of desperate illness; I knew my serenity close to death could only have been from God. But as I began to get better the dynamics changed from acute agony to tedious, ongoing pain. I bumped into how limited my recovery was. 'Better' meant improved, not well. It meant being imprisoned by pain. Where was the light in *that* darkness? How could a life like that see Christ's love or reflect His light?

I know that I am not alone. Others – many others – in this life long only for release. They feel utterly entrenched in and surrounded by their own form of pain – physical or other.

Last month, a lady whom I knew a little suddenly collapsed. Within a fortnight, she had died. At the funeral I watched her husband and three teenage children. Their faces, though mourning, were serenely radiant. They were confident that Sylvia was now with her Lord, in a place where she knew no more pain, no more tears.

'I mustn't long for that,' I told myself. I clenched my fists tightly inside my coat pocket.

I looked at the wooden coffin. It was as if it were insignificant; nothing. It reminded me of a book I had read in which the Little Prince had described a dead body. 'Like an old abandoned shell,' he had said. 'There is nothing sad about old shells . . .'

No, there was nothing sad about Sylvia's dead body. Those who were left were sad in their loss, of course, but not Sylvia. She had only gained. It was not the coffin which was difficult for me to look at. It was myself.

I was still encased in my body, my pain. I was like that Little Prince before his death. He had said, 'I cannot carry this body with me. It is too heavy.' That was how I felt too.

That day, I felt particularly burdened by the heaviness of my body. I did not realise it then, but I was heading for another bout of peritonitis. It was less than a week since I had seen a new specialist in London. I had hoped that as a result of this consultation a new treatment might be suggested to alleviate the worsening symptoms. I had thought a clever new 'bigwig' might be able to cure me.

The consultation had hardly begun before that hope was torn from me. 'You're a problem,' were the doctor's first words to me. 'What do you expect but pain, with a history like yours?'

Sylvia's funeral service was too soon after that for me. I was not able to cope with the stark comparison between the old abandoned shell in the coffin and my living body, pulsating with pain.

Throughout the service I wrestled with myself. While others wept silently in sorrow, I fought back my tears. I had to keep control. I knew that if I shed one tear, it would not be just a quiet little sniffle. I would have sobbed uncontrollably. I would have prostrated myself before my Father. I would have been beside myself; I would have wept on and on, unable to bear this focus for years of exasperation.

'I can't bear this, Lord. I can't. I *can't!*' I would have cried. 'What are you asking of me? What are you doing to me? It's too much! If pain is to be my whole life, I don't want it. I don't want life!'

And it was not just on my own behalf that I felt distraught. 'Lord, look at Matthew quietly bearing so much. When I look at his eyes, I see reflected in them the whole story of my suffering. I feel helpless. I am the main character acting out this saga, yet I have no means of altering the plot. Lord, stop it, please!'

But I didn't let go like that. Somehow, I managed to maintain some composure, some unselfish serenity. It was so hard! At that moment everything seemed hard: all my pain, life itself, even God.

And there, all the time, stood that coffin. Dead. Nothing was hard any more for that old abandoned shell. To die was gain.

I burned with the frustration that this, so nearly, had been me. Not once, but at least three times I had nearly died. I had not been afraid. Yet as we rose to sing a hymn at Sylvia's funeral, the vivid memories of those times flooded back to me with a certain horror.

The time most clearly in my mind was in 1979. On that occasion I was on the operating table in theatre. I had suddenly realised that I was able to hear all that was going on around me. Somehow I was amazingly detached, as if I were an interested observer of everything. I listened to the tense voices which surrounded me.

'She needs more oxygen.'

'Her pulse rate is very high.'

'Her blood pressure's dropped even further.'

Then a man's authoritative boom. 'Get some plasma. Quickly, nurse.' The sound of wooden clogs on the stone floor receded, running, then returned.

'Where *is* the plasma?' she had asked, flustered.

'Poor soul,' I mused, remembering my own early days as a student nurse learning the whereabouts of equipment on each ward or department.

The man's voice in reply was raised. 'I don't care where the hell it is. Just get it. Quickly!'

I felt detached from it all. I was interested in speculating why they should want the plasma so quickly for me. I also knew where the plasma was. 'On the second shelf, above the Dextrose solution,' I wanted to say helpfully. But it didn't matter. I was all right. All this was going on, but it didn't seem to affect me somehow. I felt unburdened. Why were they worrying? I felt amazingly free and light.

'She's not breathing.' It was the man's voice. What did it matter though? I felt fine.

'Blood pressure's very low. Speed up that drip.' Really, they were fussing. Certainly they couldn't have known how well I felt. They didn't seem to know that I could hear.

'Jane? Jane?' A voice calling me kept intruding upon my freedom. 'Can you take a big breath for me, Jane?' No, I couldn't. Why bother anyway? I was flying, floating, free.

'Pass my laryngoscope.' It was the man's voice again.

Suddenly my chin was jerked upwards. Fingers pressed my jaw and throat. An enormous metal instrument was being pushed into my mouth, past my tonsils. I couldn't get away from it. I couldn't shout for help.

The fiddling stopped, but their invasion into me had hardly begun. Involuntarily, I felt myself drawing breath. Or was it a breath? A heaviness fell upon me, infusing my whole being. Then, as suddenly as they had filled, my lungs emptied.

'Good,' came the voice. Good? I thought. The man was so wrong. This was not 'good'. I felt much worse now. I resented the heaviness, the burden of breathing. His interference had ended the feeling of a freedom and lightness which I had experienced for the first time ever. I resented it deeply. I felt claustrophobic, trapped, pressed in by the tubes now being tied into my mouth with a bandage around my head.

Then I heard the click-hum of another machine. As its hum crescendoed, I felt my lungs fill again. Click – hum. They emptied. A new dread came over me. With a chill I realised I had been put on to a ventilator.

In church, the hymn was almost over now. My eyes turned again towards Sylvia's family. They too knew the distinctive click – hum of a ventilator. Sylvia's breathing had needed to be assisted for a number of days before she had died.

I wanted to be able to reassure them. 'There's no terror in actually dying,' I would have said. 'You just feel ill. It's like feeling ill with flu, except that you don't get better just temporarily. Once you die you become completely whole and well, face to face with Jesus. Permanently.'

The aspect of being face to face with Jesus was very important to me. Each time I have nearly died, I have been conscious of Jesus very close to me: so close that I would hardly have been surprised if His presence had become a physical thing. He would have reached out and taken my hand. For onlookers I suppose that that would have been the moment of my death; but for me it would have been the beginning of Life in a big way.

I recalled another occasion when I had positively looked forward to Jesus coming to take
me by the hand after hearing a visiting preacher
at Matthew's theological college. This was in
February, 1980, just before my collapse, when
he had shared with the students a picture he
had seen in his mind. It was of Jesus leading 'God's daughter' into heaven as a bride.
Angels were forming a corridor as they stood
waiting to see the Bridegroom come and lead
His bride through that corridor. All the angels
were craning their necks to see the beauty of the
bride. Jesus was proud to take His bride before
His Father.

At the time of hearing this man's vision, we had
no idea of what lay ahead during the college year.
Matthew and I did know that his words had had a
very special ring of truth.

This was all immensely reassuring as we con-
templated Sylvia's death. But I found it was no
use comparing my pain with others'. Sylvia's
suffering had been so worthwhile. It had led her
to her death, when she would see God face to
face. She could be thankful even for the actual
pain, because it was acting as a vehicle to carry
her to the place where God would 'wipe away
every tear'.

But for me? The prophetic words, speaking of
the release of death into fullness and wholeness of
life, seemed to heighten the distress of living on,
burdened by so much pain.

Sylvia's release caused me to long for God's
nearness, for the promise of a wonderful, per-
manent future. It was quite easy for me to be
convinced by the truth that 'to die is gain'. My

gain would be eternal. It was much more difficult, however, to welcome the other half of that verse, 'For me to live is Christ . . .'. It was a struggle to understand how to find Christ in my life, when life involved so much pain and suffering.

I found in myself a reaction near to bitterness. I had been so near to this wonderful reception in which Sylvia was rejoicing . . . and yet so far. Would it not have been a more appropriate ending to a long saga of unexplained suffering, if I had died triumphantly?

But that is not what God had planned. Jesus did not come to take me by the hand and lead me with joy to His Father. He did not give the release we had anticipated. Instead, he called me to stay in my shell. He called me to remain, living in pain, for we did not know how long.

Perhaps He leads us gently, but I cannot say He has always felt gentle to me. The jolt of realising that He wants me to face this second-best place, on earth, can still be devastating. At such times, I desperately need to be reassured by God Himself that His way and His timing are perfect.

And yet the paradox is that the light shines in the darkness. Once, I received exactly such reassurance. Lying in hospital one day in 1980, semi-conscious, semi-drugged, I suddenly became aware of a great clarity of mind. I knew without doubt that the thoughts in my head were very important. Reaching for a pen and scrap of old tissue paper I began to write, phrase by phrase. I did not know the next sentence until I had written the first.

God was directly giving me His words of comfort for the darkness which was to follow:

You long for death because that is where you know He'll be. In fact the end is also the end of your resources – where you cannot cope, you cannot bear any more. That is where I am, but usually you do not feel Me there because of the intensity of your awareness of the end – that state where you are 'dead' to God, to Me.

Therefore, prepare yourself for this end, first of all by recognising that it exists – that you will feel desperate and that you will be lonely. Then, while you are cool and rational, see ahead that I will be there. Don't think this will be a blueprint for Me to act, or be seen to act, when the darkness comes. Only, when it comes, remember that this is the end of your coping, and that that is where I take over, silently, without you even knowing.

You cannot long for this end of being able to cope because it is too dreadful, too dark. But be reassured to know that that is where you meet more fully with Me, even though it's in a subconscious way. Just because it's subconscious and unfelt (as opposed to your physical death which will be as exciting as your wedding day) it's no less real to Me. So, Jane, I do not expect you to look forward to these times, or to look back on them with joy. But you needn't dread them so much, knowing that I understand. Remember my hour in Gethsemane?

Arriving home after Sylvia's funeral, I raced upstairs. I thumbed through my drawer of precious pieces of paper until I found these words. Hungrily, I read them over and over again. Yes, today was one of those times about which God had spoken. I felt at the end of my resources, unable to cope.

But Christ was not only to be found in death. I relaxed a little as I opened my mind to the idea that God was nonetheless with me. This was His promise, His absolute assurance, however hard that felt for me to believe. The gospel does not simply say that God can rescue me out of my suffering. He can rescue me in it. If it was God's will for me to live, then Christ was to be found there as well.

Kneeling beside my Bible, I turned to the Beatitudes. 'How blest are those who know their need of God', I read from the slightly different translation of the New English Bible. That was me all right; I knew my need of God. 'The kingdom of Heaven is theirs.'

Then there was my favourite Psalm. 'As the deer pants for streams of water, so my soul pants for you, O God' (Psalm 42:1). These verses certainly summarised my longing. But I needed more. I needed to hear some words of love, of tenderness, from God. Turning to the book of Isaiah, I began to read from chapter 43. I lifted my head and closed my eyes. I tried to absorb the love of God as I pondered His word.

To trust this verse was, I was sure, the only way I could endure living here on earth, in pain. If I could really receive this verse as God Himself speaking to me here and now, I would be able to know without doubt not only that 'to die is gain', but also, 'to live is Christ'.

In silence I remained kneeling, alone before God, allowing His word to speak to me personally.

'You are precious, and honoured in my sight, and I love you.'

5

'You are precious'

(Isaiah 43:4)

It was August 1980 and I was much stronger after my operation. I was eagerly looking forward to another visit to a convent where Matthew and I had spent three helpful weekends the previous year. The 'total pelvic clearance' six weeks previously had served to stop the downward spiral of my illness and I was gradually regaining health and strength. However, there was still something lacking. Life was not wonderful. I had no enthusiasm to enter into life fully, and I did not understand why.

When we arrived at the convent in Hertfordshire, I felt happy enough. We were warmly welcomed by the five Carmelite sisters whom we had come to know during our earlier visits. They were the Sisters of the Love of God, who saw their calling as spreading God's love throughout the world in prayer. They each sought to let God's love be made bigger in themselves. That love certainly spread to us in the welcome we received. As they showed Matthew and myself to our separate little rooms

I was full of anticipation that our three days there would help me to feel restored in every way.

We discussed only a few details about the silent meals and other practical matters before the sisters returned to their own contemplative work. Then, as Sister Rachel-Mary graciously left me in order to 'allow me to enjoy the peace and stillness', she closed my door.

Suddenly I felt terribly alone. I had expected to find quietness, rest and peace in the silence. Instead, I found confusion. My mind was full of thoughts all clamouring loudly for my attention.

What was wrong with me? I had made good progress and was well on the way to recovery. I had been seriously ill, on the brink of dying, but I had come through. Why was my heart not full of praise and thankfulness to God? Surely I ought to be rejoicing with all those who had prayed for this healing?

Dissatisfied with myself for not being able to find peace even in so quiet a place, I decided to take a stroll in the extensive grounds. Perhaps being outside would take me out of myself, away from the drab simplicity of my room.

I sat down on a wooden bench beside the fish pond. The water glistened in the summer sun. To the right and behind, the kitchen garden stretched down the slope, all methodically laid out with vegetables. Beyond, huge brown nets enclosed further neat rows of fruit bushes. Everything I saw was ordered and calm. Closing my eyes to enjoy the sun's balmy rays, I tried to absorb some of this peacefulness. I heard the sound of the bird-song, interrupted only by the gentle scratching noise of a sister hoeing the well-tilled earth.

I thought back to one of my previous visits to the convent. I had been very pleased with life then. I had been on the crest of a wave with my achievements. I had just been appointed to a good position as a nursing sister doing research. The post had combined both academic and clinical work, alongside the university professor and two consultants. This early promotion stood me in very good stead for my career.

I had also won a national award made by the Royal College of Nursing for an essay, and had been made to feel very important as a special guest at a cocktail party in the lavish rooms of the Royal College in London. The award had led to a contract to write a nursing textbook. At the age of twenty-four I felt thrilled and honoured. I seemed to have a valuable contribution to make in life. Through my achievements, I felt that my life was worthwhile and that therefore I was precious.

I reflected how much my thinking had changed during that particular weekend at the convent. Having arrived so full of self-worth, I was brought up with a jolt on the first morning. A note had been pushed under my door. I recognised the handwriting to be Mo's. She was another student who had come with us from Matthew's college. She had copied one simple poem for me to meditate upon during the course of our silence:

I wait for you my child.
I desire your love
More than anything else you can give me.
Not your service
    Not your struggling and trying to please Me,
Or to please others.

I want you to love me;
To love Me with all your heart, mind, soul,
    strength.
This is the first commandment
And matters more than all else besides.
I need your love, fellowship, devotion and
    worship.
I want you to be single-minded in this one
    thing.
My Spirit is within you
To enable you
To empower you
To fill your heart with love.

I desire this not sometimes
But always.

The poem had absolutely stopped me in my tracks.
It suggested to me that God would be more pleased
to see my relationship with Him deepen, than to
see me doing wonderful things with my God-given
talents. 'I desire your love more than anything else
you can give me' – more, even, than my achievements for Him. Who I was was more important to
Him than what I did or achieved in life.

As I recalled that previous stay in the convent,
something seemed to slot into place in my mind.
Could it be, I wondered as I got up to walk again
through the grounds, that I had allowed myself
to forget the lessons I had learned through Mo's
poem? Had I been lulled back into the way our
society thinks of people's worth, and away from
God's perspective? That would certainly explain
why I felt unhappy with my own company. In strong
contrast to the high sense of self-esteem I enjoyed

then, I did not now have any 'achievements' to be pleased about. I had spent the past six months passively enduring illness. During that time I had had no chance to 'earn' any feeling of being special in life. Unlike my last visit here, I now had no outward measure that I was precious.

A bell tolling softly interrupted my musings. Slowly I strolled back up the slope towards the chapel. But my mind did not enter into the ten-minute chanted office. I was relieved, too, as we filed into lunch directly afterwards, that the rule of silence meant that I was not expected to join in with any polite conversation.

I chose a seat in the dining-room from which I could gaze out to the garden. I felt that that would raise my spirits. Nature seemed so uncluttered by the burdens which appeared to weigh me down.

I recalled one very vivid memory of being told that I was precious, not by words, but by tears. It was during the four-month crisis earlier in the year. A very dear friend, Jennie, had once again left her young baby in order to journey in to be with me. She had known how ill I was and had wanted to show how much she cared.

The day she came was one of my worst. I was so distracted by the burning intensity of pain that I had lost my way around the all-too-familiar ward. I had lost control of bodily functions. The Sister had summoned the consultant out of theatre to come to me, because she knew I was going downhill. By the time he had come, I had been unable to respond to his questions. I had just stared through him, as indeed I did to Jennie when she arrived later.

It was a crucial time: the time when, I suspect, I was giving up my drive to get well. The consultant,

I was later told, was himself distraught about my condition, probably because he knew that no medical man can stop a patient giving up her spirit. He recognised how I felt. He described me as being 'on a downward spiral'. He knew that I could bear very little more. I was utterly spent. That day, I was simply giving up.

Jennie did not try to cajole me out of my mood with philosophical reasons to live. She simply wept. She must have sensed immediately how I was, and how I felt; for even as she took her coat off I remember seeing her face dissolve. She dragged the nearest chair to be close beside me, took my unresponsive hand in both of hers, and sobbed. She buried her face in her hands, and mine, kissing mine and stroking them as if she were handling a really valuable treasure. Though I must have been quite passive, she made me feel that I was precious.

I thank God Jennie cried as she did. Some people might have suppressed their natural reaction, trying not to add to my problems by parading their distress. But Jennie jolted me into a sudden awareness of my situation which I had lost. At the simplest level, she was so much herself that she was the first person whom I recognised that day. She helped to bring me round from my stupor.

But she did more than that. Her tears showed me that she cared. She caused the first stirrings in me to turn back from my only desire at that moment, which was to avoid more pain. Jennie could see that I had given up fighting, and clearly she longed to see me retrieve some spark of life. She valued me here. By her tears, she told me that my life *was* worthwhile.

This memory was at the same time consoling

to me and upsetting. I was consoled to think of Jennie's indisputable love; yet I was perturbed to find that I almost wanted to repeat the whole scene so that I could feel reassured thus once again.

Watching a squirrel darting up a tree outside, I felt I was beginning to understand why I was not particularly thankful to have been saved from dying in hospital. The trouble was, I did not really believe that I was precious – precious to God, precious in the world. Stripped of all worldly reassurance that I was making a valuable contribution to life, now it was apparent that I had lost my sense of self-worth. The spiritual lessons I thought I had learned from Mo's poem were merely words: head knowledge and not heartfelt conviction. God's words of comfort did not really comfort me! I had lost touch with the reality of His pronouncement, 'You are precious and honoured, and I love you.' I reacted by saying to God in a rather embarrassed way, 'Oh, that's nice of You.' But I did not feel any different.

I glanced across to Matthew, eating awkwardly from his wooden bowl which each person used at the convent. What was he thinking, I wondered? He, more than anyone else, was caught up in the cost of my being alive: he was the one who supported me so strongly throughout both the crises and the long-term, residual pain. Yet he had never once suggested that the value of my life was not worth the pain, even though he too was caught up in that cost. He did not feel, as I did, that my life was just a burden.

My eyes filled with tears as I thought once again of the burden I felt myself to be: a burden both to myself, enduring pain and feeling unwell, and to others who had to endure my limitations and my moans.

Suddenly I was aware of Sister Rachel-Mary looking at me. I had been so lost in thought that I had forgotten that I was with others. But it was too late.

There was a gentle knock on the door of my room later in the afternoon. I knew then that Sister Rachel-Mary had noticed the signs of my low spirits. She sat on my bed as she asked how I was.

'I don't know,' was my lame reply. 'I just don't know.' I was too bewildered to be objective about myself.

'You've been through a great ordeal,' she said with conviction. 'A lot has happened to you physically. You need time to catch up emotionally and spiritually.'

I smiled and relaxed a little. It was an enormous relief to be accepted so fully. Sister Rachel-Mary was very perceptive and wise. I felt able to trust her with what was weighing so heavily on my heart.

'I know I ought to be grateful to God for healing me,' I began tentatively. 'But I just don't feel glad to be alive.'

Sister Rachel-Mary frowned a little. 'Like a death wish, you mean?'

'No. I don't actively want to die. I'm feeling much more passive than that. I just lack any enthusiasm for living.'

'But you've been profoundly weakened, Jane: not just physically, but in every way. Anyone is bound to feel like this after being as ill as you have been, quite apart from the pain you're still having to combat every day. You're a strong person. You expect yourself to dance through everything, but you are setting yourself goals which are too high.' Her eyes twinkled affectionately.

Comforted a little by her reassurance, I dared to explain further.

'It's not just that, though. This morning I realised that I don't feel that I'm special.' I could not say more, for fear that my voice might reflect my nearness to breaking down.

'Aren't you allowing yourself to forget all the signs from other people who have shown you how special you are to them? You yourself have written that to me in your letters.'

She was right. People had reached out to me in many different ways: from those who sent simple but caring messages by card or with flowers, to those who gave up whole weeks of their time to help run the house.

'Yes, that has helped. But it doesn't stop my underlying feeling that I am now thoroughly restricted in what I can do in life. I mean, it wouldn't really have mattered if I were not in the world. If I had died when we expected me to – well, everyone would have been sad, but they would have got over it. Life would have gone on without me. So, is it important that I am still here? What does it mean, "You are precious"?'

I looked at her doubtfully, but her bowed head signalled that she was ready to listen to more.

'Because as far as I am concerned, it means telling myself, "Keep going, Jane. God says it's worth your being alive so you've got to trust Him. Keep battling through pain. You must endure suffering patiently." But it's hard . . . it's so hard.' And my voice trailed away.

There was a silence between us; but I knew that Sister Rachel-Mary was not dependent on words for communication. The serenity in her face encouraged me to open up more fully.

'The trouble is, I suppose, that I allow my self-esteem to be either built up or eroded by other people's images of me. I work my guts out trying to be noticed as doing well, be it at work or among friends or in the church fellowship. I enjoy giving of myself because that is very fruitful: it gives me the feedback that my role in life is appreciated, according to what I give. Being appreciated makes me feel precious.'

Sister Rachel-Mary nodded with understanding. As part of her vocation she had schooled herself in dying to her own desires and ambitions, through the three vows she had made of poverty, chastity, and obedience.

'This illness has forced me into a place where I am restrained from giving as I would like. I am forced instead to receive. You mentioned just now about all the care I've been shown. Perhaps people imagine that I must feel precious because I receive so much kindness from those who want to minister to me. But I'm so accustomed to "earning" my feeling of being precious that I find it difficult to stop giving and simply, passively, to receive.'

Already I was feeling better for talking all this out. I could almost guess her 'answer' before Sister Rachel-Mary spoke.

'But our Lord does not think of importance and special-ness as we do. He wants us to learn that we are precious to Him in whatever state we are in. He values us for who we are in the quietness of our soul.'

I was silenced, at last, by the wisdom of her words. Then, before leaving me to rest once more, Sister Rachel-Mary asked me to think about a verse. I knew it well: Psalm 46, verse 10, 'Be still and know that I am God.'

'Spend time with it,' she said confidently. 'It may well help you now.'

I thought at first that it was rather an obvious verse for her to quote to me. What else was I doing at the convent other than being still? Yet I admired Sister Rachel-Mary greatly, and I knew that after her years of a close pilgrimage with her Lord, anything she said was worth my taking seriously.

Whatever I did, I held the verse in my mind . . . brushing my teeth, eating my meals, kneeling quietly before the cross in the little chapel. The next day in my reading I found a Latin translation of the same verse. '*Vacete et videte*' – 'Vacate, make empty, and see . . .' I looked pensively to the huge log fire beside me.

'So,' I told myself, 'this is the key. I've to empty out all the things which lead to my self-satisfaction, and count them as trash instead of treasures. God is not interested in my achievements. I've to come to Him with nothing. He wants only me, in my emptiness. Only then can He do what He wills in me.'

During the following months I kept these thoughts uppermost in my mind. I found myself much less despondent whenever I was faced with the limitations set by the continuing low-level pain. Then at Christmas time, another dear friend confirmed my thoughts about 'doing' and 'being'. Sally wrote in her Christmas letter: 'In writing this letter about the "doings" of the year, one is tremendously aware that these are only the icing on the cake, and that the all-important work is that of the Spirit of God working within our lives.'

As I look back, I know that the Spirit of God, working within me, has taken away much of my 'doing'. He has worked like a gardener pruning a valuable plant or tree, in that He has not merely cut out dead or useless growth: He has also cut me where I have been fruitful and growing healthily. This is exactly what Jesus said, 'Every branch that does bear fruit He prunes, that it may bear more fruit.'

To find areas of my life being cut out by God has sometimes been hard. At times I have felt that He has been so ruthless in His pruning, and it has hurt so much, that I could not be precious to Him. But I know that that is not true. Again, it is a poem which has helped me to see beyond the hurt of what God has taken away from me, and to trust that He has a loving purpose:

It is the branch that bears the fruit
    that feels the knife
To prune it for a larger growth,
    a fuller life . . .

It is the hand of Love Divine
    that holds the knife,
That cuts and breaks with tenderest touch,
That thou, whose life has borne some fruit
    May'st now bear much.

Whatever pain my Father has asked me to endure is not worthless or without a loving purpose – however unloving it all seems at times. I should not be surprised, nor should my faith waver, when some fruitful area of my life is cut away. But that is easier for me to write about than to endure. No amount of acceptance diminishes the dreadful reality of suffering.

Sometimes it is hard to discern when the Spirit of God is at work, and where His enemy is endeavouring to destroy. They may both want to cut away fruitful areas of my life, but for very different reasons. My Father only takes something away in order to make room for fuller growth. His enemy would want me to become bitter, resentful and self-pitying.

I have needed to trust my Father never to cut anything out of my life except with loving hands which tend the wounds where He has pruned. His purpose is never to destroy because, He says clearly, 'you are precious'. He cares for me. I know this, though if I am honest I have to admit that I do not, as yet, really feel the tenderness of His love.

The practical outworking of the Spirit of God within our lives can seem very, very hard. Often, I have sung the hymn,

> Spirit of the living God
> Fall afresh on me . . .
> Break me, melt me,
> Mould me, fill me . . .

God has answered, and He continues to answer, that prayer-song. He has broken me, and when I have felt the pain of being broken I have reflected on how much easier it is to sing the song than to accept the brokenness.

God has used physical suffering to break me. There are many little reminders in day-to-day life which cause me to think of my body's brokenness and incompleteness. When I see the scars from twelve abdominal operations, I am reminded that my physical brokenness also represents a brokenness of my Spirit. Through physical surgery, God has 'opened me up' and shown me parts of myself which I may have preferred not to see.

The smallest little thing occasionally reminds me that part of my womanhood has been taken away. For some years, whenever I saw the sales machines in ladies' toilets, for example, I felt slightly less of a woman. I knew I should have been counting my blessings and I was glad of the freedom I had each month, but I also felt left out, incomplete, broken.

God calls all of us to be broken, just as He was broken. In the upper room, Jesus took a whole loaf of bread and broke it into pieces, as a dramatic illustration of what happened to His body. And He asks His disciples to follow Him.

God has melted me. I expect I would have welcomed a nice gentle heat to make me aglow with His Spirit, but that would not have been hot enough to melt me. Instead, He has put me through a great burning intensity of heat, just as gold has to be put into a white-hot furnace in order to be melted. When the fire of purification has felt so hot, so painful, I have often wondered why I ever asked God to melt me. Yet I know (in my head) that God has only done this because He values me. He is interested in the quality of my life and He purifies me in the fire – because I am precious.

Looking back, I can see clearly that God has

melted away lots of rubbish from my life, and that however unbearable, His fire has strengthened my faith just as Peter wrote, 'your faith [is] of greater worth than gold, which perishes even though refined by fire' (1 Peter 1:7). I trust that He has done this in order to remould me.

God is moulding me, and in being moulded I have had to learn to be pliable so He can reshape me as He wants. He keeps on and on, just as a potter persists at his clay. I know that with each successive bout of illness I change a little, as God knocks off another sharp edge from me; but sometimes I feel tired and dizzy going round the potter's wheel. I look at those who do not seem to be having such a hard time, and fall into the trap of self-pity.

Yet I do know that God does not delight in causing His little ones to suffer. He continues to mould me because He is delighted to create vessels according to His design. I am beginning to learn not to wish that I could jump off the wheel, but to give myself more to His hands. I am beginning to pray honestly, 'Keep turning Your wheel today, so that Your hands can mould me as You desire.'

Being broken, melted and moulded leaves a vessel which is ready to be filled. At the convent, God convicted me that my value in life to Him lies *in my emptiness*. I knew then that I can only be filled by Him when I make space for Him, which means emptying myself. The Holy Spirit has had the hard work to do in me, of breaking my strong exterior, melting me to the core, and moulding me. All His work, which continues, has been in order to fill me.

God has filled me, quietly and undramatically. I know that at times I would have preferred to remain filled than to dare to pray, again and again, for the hurt of being broken, melted, and moulded. But God yearns for me to keep growing, to keep being filled. He wants to keep working in me, because I am precious.

I constantly need to keep readjusting my perspectives. So much of what I see around me threatens to deceive me with the lie that it is a person's achievements that give him value. Consequently I begin to fear that the debilitating aspects of my suffering rob me of my worth. But God views things differently. He loves me for who I am more than for what I can do. And if it was that my very pain forced me into discovering this deep truth, then surely I should embrace it rather than despise it?

However, there is a tension to be held between this truth and the fact that God is the One who, looking with compassion on His suffering people, said with authority, 'Be healed'.

6

'Be healed'

(Mark 5:34)

I know that God is able to take away all pain. I have read about His miracles while He was on earth and I have seen His power at work in others. So, I wondered, couldn't He decide to intervene in my suffering, and use His great healing power to put an end to all my pain?

Once I was told very clearly, 'You must thank God that He has already healed you.' I had just been prayed for by a man who was well known by Christians around the world for the powerful gift of healing. Four of us had come to Matlock, to see and hear him, and possibly to seek ministry through the laying on of hands.

I had hesitated about going. I knew, partly, that I would be going for the wrong reasons – I was intrigued to see this man and to witness some of the famous signs and wonders associated with his ministry. 'But then,' I consoled myself, 'while Jesus was on earth, people like Zacchaeus often went to observe Him out of curiosity before they could trust

Him. If Jesus accepted their mixed motives, I'm sure God will accept me if I draw near to Him, for whatever initial reason I go.'

But this was only a small part of my hesitancy. There was much more than that; something which went much deeper. The trouble was, I knew what had gone before. I was almost embarrassed to recall just how often I had been forward at healing services. I had had the laying on of hands so many times, by so may people. I had been prayed over and even anointed with oil by several men of God including (for what it was worth) two wonderful bishops. Was it right for me to go yet again? Was I seeking something magical in this man? Because if so, was I not in danger of 'worshipping' the man, rather than God Himself? If it had been God I was seeking, was He not the same God, equally able to hear me and heal me whoever laid hands on me?

Did I need to go again to ask for healing? Had God not heard me the first time? By asking for the same thing each time, was I actually evading God's response? I had an uncomfortable inkling that maybe He could have been trying hard to give me an answer, that He had some purpose in withholding physical healing.

If I went that evening, wasn't I just trying yet another key in the lock? As if healing were like a gift in a locked cupboard, available only to those who had the right key? That seemed to contradict how I thought of God. I did not think it was in His nature to withhold something good, just because I did not pray in the 'right' way with the 'right' words. After all, Jesus had despised the Pharisee's 'right' form of prayer and had honoured the genuineness of the simple, humble prayer: 'Lord, have mercy on me, a sinner!'

I laid aside all these questions, and more. I had been persuaded to go. I must have been desperate. At any cost, I wanted to be completely free of pain. Physical pain lingered on even though the crisis in 1980 was now over and I had recently returned to work. Psychologically I was still in pain, too, fighting against the haunting memories of the severe physical symptoms I had had to endure. And emotionally, it was a struggle to resume my enthusiastic work as a midwife after my own hysterectomy. I had chosen to do so; I wanted to overcome; I was determined not to be defeated by it – but it was still a struggle. Still a form of pain.

'Just think what you might be missing,' said Alastair and Alison as they urged me to accompany them. 'Swallow your pride and come on.'

The idea that it might be sheer pride which was stopping me from drawing near to God was the final straw. Dragging Matthew along with us, we jumped into the car all together.

By the end of the evening I came away asking myself what that man had meant telling me to 'thank God that He had already healed' me? Because it sounded as if he was telling me to have more faith than I had. It is only after years of pondering, ruthlessly questioning myself, others, God Himself, that I can articulate anything of how mistaken I know such an idea to have been.

At first my searching seemed completely fruitless. The first glimpse I had of the impact of that man's philosophy came much later when Matthew began his ministry as a curate in Beverley. During our four years there, I came to know a lively girl named Carol. She was a teacher who was full of character and laughter. At twenty-five years old she was only a little younger than myself. Then, soon after we first met, she was diagnosed as having multiple sclerosis.

Carol was shattered. Such a diagnosis was to affect her whole way of living and she was asking some heart-searching questions. Suddenly we had a lot in common. Very early in our friendship our conversations were deep and brutally honest.

One evening we sat together at a church meeting. I noticed that Carol lacked her usual sparkle and her eyes seemed distant and sad.

'How are you?' I asked, but not until I was putting my coat on ready to leave.

'Fine, thanks.'

I knew that answer very well. I had used it countless times myself.

'Rubbish!' I retorted, but with a smile. Carol looked up at me and broke into laughter at herself. She enjoyed being teased like a normal person, rather than constantly being pitied about her health. Her face softened with relief that she had been understood a little without needing to go through the wearisome task of explaining her complex feelings to me.

'It is rubbish, I know,' she said at last. 'I've wanted so much to talk to you. I've even tried writing to you several times, but each time the letter has ended up in the waste-paper basket.'

I sat down again beside her. I did not mind if we were the last people to leave the meeting – Carol needed to talk. I knew how hard I found it to dare to pull down my cheerful façade of saying I was 'fine, thanks'. This was the first time Carol had begun to let go with me and I did not want to let her down.

'Is it the MS itself which is getting you down?' I asked.

Carol shook her head. 'Well, partly, I suppose. The symptoms are getting worse. I can't see properly now: everything has a double image so I keep crashing into doors or walls, thinking that they are in a different place from where they are. And I'm also having "accidents" sometimes and I have to wear pads; but waterproof pants make a rustling noise which is awful. Not the sort of thing to help one to make friends quickly! I get the most amazing looks from some folk, you know.'

I sensed that underneath her apparent light-heartedness, Carol was feeling very low. There was nothing I could say. No solution, no answer. Just, 'I'm sorry.' At least she knew I meant it.

Carol ventured to trust me a little further. 'The thing is, while I'm acquiring these extra problems related to the MS, everyone I love and trust seems to be convinced that I will be healed, and soon. I feel I'm under immense pressure.'

'Pressure from other people's expectations, you mean?'

'Mmmm. Almost unbearable at times . . .' Carol looked away pensively before continuing, 'Don't get me wrong – it would be lovely and I would be an idiot not to ask God for healing and expect it.'

Carol and I had both witnessed recently the quiet miracle in our church of David, whose crippling arthritis had been healed when he was twenty-two. Neither of us had any doubts that God does heal today. Yet Carol's experience in her own suffering was different. She explained, 'For example, last time I was at a healing service it was particularly difficult for me. I felt everyone in the room was expecting me to be healed, and if I wasn't then the fault could only be mine.'

'How can people say that?' I uttered, more to myself than to Carol. The question was rhetorical but Carol answered nevertheless.

'Oh, Jane, you know perfectly well how their argument goes: that God wants to heal, He wants His children to be healthy, and we have only to ask.'

'Yes, I've had all that said to me,' I replied. My mind went straight back to that meeting in Matlock when I had been told to 'thank God that He had already healed' me. I was almost tired of hearing it. 'Quite honestly I often get the feeling that it's easier for people to say that than to go a bit deeper. They can remain untouched by the pain of long-term suffering if they give a quick solution to it.'

'But how do you cope with people who try to help like this? Are they right? Oh, I'm so confused.'

I thought for a moment. It perturbed me to see that Carol had been upset, especially by those who tried to help, but I hardly knew where to start. There was no simple answer.

I began gently. 'Well, it didn't take long for me to realise that it isn't always as simple as some people suggest. If, as you say, we "only have to ask", then without a doubt I would have been healed a long time ago. But I wasn't.'

Carol answered quickly, 'No, so you have to have faith, don't you? People say that it's my lack of faith that's stopping me from being healed.'

I felt my frustration rising. I found it very hard to remain patient when people gave such a glib explanation as that.

'How much faith do they think you need?' I asked hotly. 'Because if you look in the Bible, Jesus said all you need is faith the size of a grain of mustard seed. That's enough to move a mountain. Some Christians can make you feel utterly condemned if your faith isn't the size of a melon! But that's other people, not God. A mustard seed is enough for God. Have you got that much faith?'

Carol giggled. 'Yes, I have!' She seemed pleased to have some assurance that she was not so completely feeble a Christian as she had been caused to feel, at least not on that score.

'In any case,' I continued, 'people who say your healing depends on you having enough faith should read Hebrews. In among the long list of heroes who are examples of those with faith, there's a little verse . . .' I fumbled to find Hebrews chapter 11. 'It says, "These were all commended for their faith, yet none of them received what had been promised. God had planned something better . . ."' I looked at Carol, whose forehead was puckering.

'What on earth does that mean?' she asked.

'It means that if we fail to receive what God has promised (like healing), we can take heart. We can be sure He has something better for us. Pressing on *without* receiving is actually commended! According to the person who wrote Hebrews, that is an evidence of faith.'

Carol sighed ruefully. 'Oh, it would be nice if things were that way round.'

'I think it *is* that way round – when God chooses

for it to be.' I became very quiet before adding, 'I want to hold on to that hope.'

After a moment my voice became a little harder. 'Anyway, if they are so impressed about the need for faith, you should remind them about Jairus' daughter, or the centurion's servant. It was the faith of the friends, and not the sufferer's faith, which impressed Jesus.'

Carol was obviously not ready to detach herself enough from the pressure of her friends to share my laughter. She went on, 'They tell me adamantly that I will be fully fit very soon.'

My cheeks flushed as I saw how people sometimes manage to avoid facing up to suffering. How much easier it was to say that Carol would be healed, than to think she might not be. She was so bright and vivacious – how could God let her become crippled?

I burst out, 'How can they be adamant? Have they asked God? Do they know the mind of Christ? Usually those who genuinely do have His mind are humble, not adamant. Have they given time to listen to God – specifically about you and your MS? How, exactly, did it come to them that this is God's will for you?'

I could have gone on, but the glint in Carol's eye helped to stem the flow of indignation, despite the fact that I meant every word I had said.

'You often talk about seeking God's will,' Carol prompted me, her gentle tone switching from my strong outburst.

'Yes, I do. It's something which I learned a lot about while staying at a convent. I saw that for the nuns there, prayer is not telling God what you want, but opening yourself to what He wants in you. For me, that takes much more faith. It means spending time silently seeking His will. I think that the only time when, as your adamant friends say, we "just have to ask" for healing is when we know God's will for each particular person.'

Carol nodded thoughtfully. 'But according to them, I'm not the one to know God's will. You see, you've just reminded me. They say that my lack of faith makes a wall between me and my MS, and God and His healing.'

I sighed at the effect of such advice on someone like Carol whose suffering made her so vulnerable to their opinions.

'You *have* been confused, haven't you?' As I reached out to touch Carol's arm, trying to convey my care, her eyes moistened. I so much wanted to comfort her, to assure her of how graciously God accepted her even when others seemed only to find faults.

'No words or arguments can help when anyone's feeling as you are now. Only you and God know if there's a wall between you. Don't rely on me or on anybody else. Just trust your own relationship with God. When you go home, why don't you try to find peace on your own with Him? Try to look at Him and be aware of Him looking to you. You will know if there is a wall between you. And if there isn't, take courage not to let others make you feel guilty.'

Carol nodded, sniffing back her tears. 'Yes, that will help,' she conceded, reaching round for her coat.

We walked towards the door and I thought out loud, 'The old devil would be thrilled if he could get at you. He knows it's hard for you to reject what loved ones say. Only, sometimes you must.'

I went home in a pensive mood. That night it was hard to sleep. It was all very well for me to have talked to Carol as I had, but I remembered times when I had felt hurt as she was now. Deeply hurt. I thought of how often I had found myself alone after visitors had left me, feeling as if it was all my own fault that I was not better. People may have meant kindly, but I'm sure they could not have realised how devastated I was by some of their advice.

The sorts of things they said went round and round my head as I tossed and turned in bed. 'I've just been reading Matthew's Gospel where Jesus says, "Ask and you will receive."' (How often I had heard that!) 'Well, presumably, Jane, you can't have asked Him properly?'

Not asked – pleaded! Besought. Hammered at His door. Wept. Cried out. Thrown myself at His feet. If He hadn't heard me, He was not the God whom I knew I could trust.

I remembered with some measure of shame, one time when a man I shall call Mike had got in touch with me. We did not know each other well but he had heard about my illness at his church. He had been concerned and, as well as praying for me, he had also wanted to do something tangible to help. He had decided to visit me at home.

I had found the time with him very tense. None of his 'helpful' suggestions was new to me, though he was clearly very enthusiastic about each one. Unfortunately (and this was where I felt somewhat ashamed as I recalled the scene) I did not have the mental energy to be more than blunt in my replies.

'You should pray in Jesus' name.'

'I always do.'

'Why don't you call together the elders of the church for laying on of hands – as in James 5?'

'I have. Lots of times.'

'You should be anointed with oil.'

'I have been.'

'You need to find out if there's something in your past which is preventing you from being healed.'

'I went to a Christian psychiatrist, with Matthew, to pursue that one. After two sessions, she described me as pretty well balanced with fairly usual sorts of hang-ups. She stopped because, she said, there was nothing abnormally wrong to cause sickness.'

'You ought to go to such-and-such a man. He has a healing ministry.'

'I went last year.'

I wanted him to see that no one formula had 'worked'. I had done all the things he was suggesting and was still left in pain. I was trying – ungraciously, I know – to make him realise that although his mind was fixed on physical healing, there was an alternative to the way in which he was talking.

Finally, he had sighed, exhausted. 'Then you must have been healed. You should thank God.'

There was that phrase again! At that point in the conversation my hands were clutching a hot-water bottle under the duvet, as I tried to find something to soothe the pain searing through me. There had been a time, years before, when I would have wondered if it were just my imagination that I was still in great pain when someone was telling me that I had been healed. But not this time.

I had felt so strongly that Mike was barging in on a delicate subject, that I had not wanted to give him my time. Yet in the end God's graciousness prevailed and I did try to explain a little.

'My first reaction to this pain continuing on and on was to think, like you now, that praying for healing was something I must do correctly in order to get what I wanted,' I told him. 'When I clearly "failed", I was caused to start thinking in a completely different way about prayer.'

Mike looked at me suspiciously. I prayed silently, asking God to help me to stay patient and be honest.

'When I pray now, I concentrate very much less on *what* I am actually asking for. I am sure He wants us to seek more of *who* He is. Only then can He reveal how to pray about specific things.'

Mike's face furrowed. I was risking a lot by trying to explain myself. I was laying myself open to accusations or criticism about my own spiritual journey. Could he understand me, I wondered? My prayer life was a personal matter and I knew that I should not mind what anyone else thought about it, but even so I felt open to Mike's judgement.

I tried to explain. 'One of the nuns at a convent I once visited put it much better than I can. She said, "Prayer is not an easy way of getting God to do things for you, but a difficult way of allowing Him to do things in you." '

'Isn't that just playing with words?' asked Mike suspiciously. 'What's the difference?'

'The difference is in the answer we seek. The "answer" to prayer is not in receiving a gift, but in meeting the Giver.'

I realised that I was trying to condense into one

conversation all that God had been teaching me over many years. Healing was an enormous subject, of which prayer was only one part. I tried to put very simply what was uppermost in my mind.

'I believe God wants the best for us, always.'

'Right.'

'My idea of the best is healing.'

'Right.'

'But God has withheld that, despite my asking for it in all the ways I have told you. Now, I could blame myself for lacking faith, or somehow not asking in the right way. But I know that I have asked in every way I can, and not alone but with the support of many faithful Christians.'

'Yes?' Mike was not quite sure he could trust me. Again I uttered a quick prayer asking God to help me to be more concerned about speaking truthfully than about what Mike thought of me.

'Or I could blame God, saying either that He has not heard me or that He is mean, withholding something good. But I cannot do either of those things, because deep down I trust Him. I just know that He does not delight in making His children suffer.'

I had to show that I was still genuinely looking to God, despite not sharing Mike's view. I had sounded so negative when he had first arrived that he might have thought I was dismissive of God. He would have been so wrong. I know God always wants to do more for me and in me than ever I can imagine.

'So it must be something else.' I paused. I did not want to say what was so important to me if Mike was not listening properly.

'What?' he asked, interested. It had never

occurred to him that, unlike us, God Himself might actually have wanted something other than physical healing for me at that point in time.

'I can only conclude that He has not healed me physically because He has something *better* for me. I said before, my idea of the best is feeling well. But at the moment anyway, it seems that that's not God's idea of the best. He does say, "My ways are not your ways". Although this dreadful pain is not my way, or the way I would choose, it seems obvious that it's His.'

'That's very harsh, isn't it?' At least Mike was thinking about what I had said.

'No: it seems harsh and it feels harsh; but I stake everything on my faith that God is not harsh. And I am not alone in believing that, contrary to our assumptions, God is doing something better and deeper.'

'Who else says that?'

I told Mike about a letter Matthew's mother had received from a friend of hers named Peter. This man had been praying for me, without knowing me, and as he had prayed a picture had formed in his mind. He had written,

I could see the face of Christ, who was looking upon Jane in her suffering. I had been surprised that, instead of encountering pain and confusion, there had been great joy and light. Jesus was looking with desire and love upon what He saw forming and coming out of the pain. Though He was mindful of the pain, the Lord took delight in the very thing which I found hard.

I concluded by telling Mike how much that encouraged me to see my suffering more from God's point of view. It helped me to feel some of His joy.

'How could God ever *want* pain?' Mike was very puzzled.

'Oh, I don't know.' I sighed. 'I don't have all the answers. I cannot explain God. I can only tell you as much as I do know so far. And encouragements such as that letter confirm to me that it isn't folly to trust God to be doing something good, even though it feels totally grim.'

'It's very different from my starting-point,' Mike said.

'But Mike,' I argued, 'every time I have gone forward for laying on of hands for healing, the physical pain has become worse rather than better. But alongside this I have been given a huge injection of closeness to the Lord. It's as if God takes me, lifts me up and reassures me that He is doing with me just what He wills."

'And do you really thank Him for that?' Mike was pressing me very hard for realistic answers.

I paused. 'Sometimes.' I hugged the hot-water bottle more closely to myself. 'I wish I could honestly say always. If I had been healed physically, I'd have leapt up and said, "Thank you, Lord!" Well, just because I can't always see the areas which He is healing, shouldn't I still be thanking Him? I suspect that His healing in me is much deeper than anything physical.'

Mike's eyes sparkled for a second; he almost spoke but then stopped himself.

'What is it?' I asked. I was still unsure of him.

'Well . . . it's just that you reminded me of the

story of the ten lepers. They were all healed, physically. Yet nine out of ten of them danced off without even speaking to Jesus again: not even to thank Him. It seems to me – and I know I'm only an onlooker – but, well, it's quite a miracle that you've at least kept coming to Him.'

I lay back on the pillows and smiled. I no longer felt accused. At last Mike and I were communicating, rather than fighting against one another. He had understood – at least a little. He had recognised that suffering could be a vehicle for faithfulness and trust in God; he saw that it was not necessarily proof of faithlessness. The relief of that was very valuable.

What I had been trying to share with him was the acceptance to which God had brought me after the terrible crisis at Tina's college flat. I had only talked about it so directly once before, and that was to Graham. Sitting in Colin's house, waiting to go back into hospital and not knowing how long I would even live, Graham had asked me, 'Do you feel God is ignoring your pain, or that He is letting things get out of hand?'

'No.' I was sure of my answer despite the desperate anguish I felt. 'No, I don't. I may not like what He's doing; I may disagree with Him. But I've put myself in His hands and asked Him to do the best for me. I know He can heal me. But He hasn't, yet. I can trust His wisdom. While I loathe the pain itself, I refuse to be tempted to stop trusting Him. He knows best. Having asked Him to do His will I can only trust Him that what's happening to me now *is* His will.'

'How are you so sure?' Graham had asked me. I replied honestly. 'Because God is in it. It's accompanied by such peace, such an assurance of Him with me that I know it's not His mistake.'

This was my conviction. To abandon myself completely into His hands, no matter what pain that caused in me. To follow Him obediently – even to the furnace for Him to purify me; to the garden for Him to prune me, cutting back good growth and making room for even more; to the threshing-mill for Him to thrash out the wheat from the chaff. This was healing.

At the healing service in Matlock, the man crouching over me had said, 'You must thank God that He has already healed you.' Maybe he was right. But I have found that whenever I consider the kind of healing which I imagine that man meant – a freedom from all pain – I encounter problems and questions. I actually turn away from the depths of healing which God has wrought in me. I resent the pain of humility, and my trust gives way to confusion and bewilderment. God's healing is so much bigger, broader and more creative than man's limited idea of pain-free solutions.

I was beginning to appreciate that healing was something to do with being taken more deeply into God. To lose sight of that would be to lose sight of God Himself and to be cast into the desolation of crying, 'My God, my God, why have You forsaken me?'

7

'Why have you forsaken me?'

(Psalm 22:1)

Resuming normal life after a long period of illness has always signified far more to me than merely the end of convalescence. My return to work in September 1980 brought to a head my difficulty in finding a peaceful equilibrium between the enormous contrasts within me. I felt I was juggling because I was constantly trying to balance the story of my pain with that of my successes.

As soon as I was back, I was confronted again by my 'successes' in midwifery. I was popular among the patients and sought-after by the consultants. Patients did not hide their disappointment that they had not had me to look after them throughout their pregnancy and labour, and many of the staff shared openly their relief that 'at last things will be done properly again!'

It did not stop there. While I had been off work, a simple audio-visual programme which I had compiled had begun to be used in other hospitals around Britain. It was being given enthusiastic praise from other midwives, and before long I was flown down to London to receive a national award. During that trip I was commissioned to create five new films which were to be distributed around the world.

I was positively exhilarated. I had known utter brokenness in my pain, but now I was tasting again great fulfilment. Soon I was lecturing to other health professionals, first in Britain and then internationally; as far afield as Australia. Once again, I was able to enjoy the glow of achievement and satisfaction, perhaps all the more so because now I saw it in a healthier perspective.

When others looked at me, they saw a strong person. I was considered the character of the department, well known for combining efficiency with good fun. Most of the time, I myself felt confident, even elated, that things were going so well.

And yet . . . and yet. What of the pain? How did that find its place in the life of one for whom everything was going so well in so many areas? Not least among all the happy-making events surrounding us, was the news in 1982 that we would expect our first baby by adoption. Should we therefore have seen things as many of our friends did, that all this apparent 'success' was some form of compensation from on high for my pain? Was the adoption of Angus and, three years later, Philippa, the joyful beginning of what has continued to be a most wonderful gift to us – was that like the icing on the cake for us, to make up for everything?

If this is so, then my emotions have not been guided by reason. For there have been times – there still are – when it seems that no amount of good things can ever counterbalance the utter brokenness within. For years I continued to feel weak, vulnerable, torn apart either by the pain or by the memories of it.

Often my longing took the form of a subconscious craving for understanding and comfort rather than a need I could specify. At such times I failed to ask for help; it took me years even to begin to learn how to do so. Those who saw only my 'successes' did not realise my unspoken needs. And so, all too easily, times have developed when I have felt forsaken not only by others but by God Himself.

I remember one such occasion very well. Lying down to rest alone one afternoon, I was suddenly aware of the hurt, confusion and loneliness which filled my mind and soul.

I had been invited to lecture at another World Congress. After two years out of clinical work since Angus' birth, I knew I would benefit not only from the three days' stimulation and challenge but also from the luxury of being looked after in an expensive hotel.

Outwardly, everything went very well. During my first lecture on the first day I had felt inspired, and the hundreds of nurses and health visitors listening had responded enthusiastically. At one point they had burst into spontaneous applause and laughter, quickly melting my nervousness in front of so many professionals. I knew I could look forward to leading a workshop the following morning with fresh confidence.

Back in my plush hotel room that evening, I was revelling in the comfort of it all. A phone call home had given me the opportunity for a lovely chat, not only with Matthew but also with Angus, very happy. 'Did you see Princess Anne, Mummy?' was all he had wanted to know. I chuckled to myself as I lay soaking in a bath full of bubbles later that evening. As I committed the day to God, I remembered a verse in Joel which someone had once thought applied very specially to me: 'I will restore the years which the locusts have eaten.'

I had had years of being stripped of everything through my pain. But I had had much restored: my fulfilment now, my career, even a family against all the odds. I thanked the Lord for His many blessings to me and drifted off into a very contented sleep.

But the next morning I was suddenly plunged into distress. I had taken a long time to wake up completely. As often happens, the abdominal discomfort which had become 'normal' for me had been incorporated into my dreams.

This time, my dreams took me back to the time when I was first ill, in Edinburgh. Half-awake, half-dreaming, I felt as I had then – too limp to move my heavy body for myself. I was aware of my heavy breathing, of my body position stretched out completely limp on the bed. In the dream, I relived the time when my breathing had been laboured because of illness, and my limp body had been placed in a similar stretched-out position by the nurses.

It was only the faintest stirring in me which strove towards consciousness: this time because I was still mostly asleep, but in Edinburgh it had been because of the severity of the peritonitis. Overtaken by pain, I had been completely passive – all except for this one tiny stirring in me which struggled, even against my own will, to fight its way to life.

Although the anguish was only a memory, it was so vivid that I felt as if the situation were actually repeating itself in reality. But in Edinburgh, there had been consolation. I could recall now how I had been comforted. I had been visited by one of my nursing tutors, Elaine. She had drawn alongside and shown her compassion to me, even though at the time I was too weak to respond. Her caring hand had gently held my forearm. It was as simple as that.

Desperately now, I longed for a gentle caress. I was reliving the scene, but without her caring touch. I wanted so much to be able to open my eyes and be comforted. I wanted to see someone like Elaine, not only beside me physically but 'with' me in understanding, as she had been. In my sleepiness the pain was so vivid and alive; but in my semi-consciousness I also knew there was no one to help. I felt forsaken.

For as long as I could, I kept my eyes tightly closed, at least trying to envisage Elaine's care and grasp it to meet my present need. If I could not be comforted as I would have liked, then at least I would try to imagine it.

Eventually the dream faded until I could no longer hold on to it. It was just a memory. The vision of someone caring for me was just a fancy. I struggled to put it out of my mind.

All day, I felt very fragile. The pain was 'only' in my mind, I knew, yet I could not shrug it off. It was as if I was still enduring it, and therefore still had to be comforted with the sort of comfort I had experienced in my dream. I had every kind of distraction, but inside I was still hurting. As always after a dream such as that, I had to force myself to do everything. Not least, I had a workshop to lead. I had to present the right image of being competent, but deep-down I was crying.

And of course, people saw no need to comfort me. Nobody saw the pain inside me. I felt very alone. In one sense I wanted it like that: I certainly did not want to be pitied or made a fuss of.

Occasionally during the day I found myself close to tears, so crushed did I feel by bearing the memory of all the pain I had gone through. 'Don't be silly,' I told myself. 'You're not ill now; you don't need comforting.'

But pain is a peculiar thing. It often lasts psychologically for longer than clock-time. It does not always go away with reasoning or bargaining. It is a silent guest which comes and goes as it pleases.

I tried to pray. 'Lord, these memories of pain are troubling me. I feel so confused and unsettled. I yearn to be comforted. You understand better than anyone else; better even than I do. Please, You be the One to hold me and to speak reassuringly to me. Let me see Your eyes, for I know they are full of compassion. Let me feel the tenderness of Your love which I know is there.'

But He did not. It was as if He were not there. As if He had withdrawn. Physically, emotionally, even spiritually, I felt utterly forsaken.

None of the events of the day, nor of my life, could console me in the emptiness I felt. This was something at the core of my being: a child unable to see her beloved Father. It was God Himself who seemed distant. No external blessing could ever compensate for that. I was weighed down in spirit, as if under a cloud. Outward achievements only served to lure me into self-satisfaction, which dragged me even further away from the child-like place of dependence where I wanted to be.

By the time my workshop was over, I was exhausted. As soon as the mêlée of people asking me questions had disappeared, I slipped back to my room in the adjoining hotel. I had been forcing myself so much, I had to rest. With relief I drank in the soothing quietness of the beautiful hotel room, so pleasant after the constant tiring buzz of noise and chatter of the conference. I locked the door firmly and flopped on to the bed.

Once again, as soon as I closed my eyes I was straight back to that scene in Edinburgh. I could not push out of my mind the memory of my profound illness and weakness. I recalled how I had been unable even to swallow. I could almost feel again the saliva dribbling from my mouth, down the side of my cheek and on to the shoulder of that unfeminine hospital gown draped around me.

I was disturbed by all this; distressed to relive such weakness and pain. Yet, in a way, I wanted to relive it. I wanted to imagine Elaine's care once again, to feast on that recollection until I had had my fill.

I was so torn! I knew that, in the end, I would never have my fill. There was an aching void within, which could fade with time but never go away completely. Nine years had passed since I had been in hospital in Edinburgh, but still it seemed as clear in my mind as if it had been only a week before. It was useless my still seeking consolation, especially on my own as I was. It made things worse when I tried, because I became so bowed down by the memory of the pain that I just felt increasingly vulnerable and isolated, far from any comfort.

'Help me, Lord!' I moaned. 'Please help me.' I buried my head in the soft pillow.

But God was silent. There was no 'answer'. No response. I felt no different spiritually, although it was a relief for me to let the tears flow at last after the morning at the conference.

I wanted to look towards God for help, but I felt let down by Him. I was in trouble; this was one of the times when I needed Him most of all. And this was the very time He had chosen to hide His face from me.

Hardly daring to speak resentfully towards Him, instead I fumbled for my Bible and allowed the Psalmist to express my own bewildered questions:

> Why are you so far away, O Lord?
> Why do you hide yourself when we are in
>   trouble?
> (Psalm 10:1, GNB)

and

How much longer will you forget me, Lord?
    For ever? . . .
How long will sorrow fill my heart day and night?
(Psalm 13:1–2, GNB)

Strangely, I had no doubt in my mind that God was with me. I can only think that He had given me this faith; certainly I could take no credit for it myself. The frustration was knowing that He, my Father, *was* . . . but in darkness.

He was not visible. He was not where I wanted Him. He had promised to be with me always, but

I could not feel him. I knew off by heart a verse in Psalm 77: 'Your path led through the sea, Your way through the mighty waters; though your footprints were not seen.'

One reassurance to me, once I was a little calmer, was that I knew I was not alone in experiencing this darkness. I had read a little of the spiritual masters who seemed not to be surprised at this phenomenon. It seemed to be a special calling, to know Him in darkness. Sister Rachel-Mary had been very encouraging to me on one point. It was because she was one of the rare people who truly seemed to identify with this forsakenness that I could respect the wisdom of what she had once written to me:

If you are going to go deeper into a 'knowledge' of God you will be drawn into the wilderness to teach you the real meaning of faith. God does withdraw the 'knowledge' of His presence in the realm of feelings, and we have to learn that Love is of the will and not the emotions, so that we will 'love Him though He slay' us.

It is just the going on, going on, with no feedback ourselves. As and when He wills, God will give you a glimpse of the sun. There will be a break in the clouds – just enough to keep you going on again in the dark.

It may surprise you, but for myself this darkness has been the norm all the time in community until about a year ago! It all *sounds* challenging and good etc., and so it is; but it *feels* like hell (and so, I suppose, it is!).

However, there was one danger. I was aware that,

while my heavenly Father could withdraw Himself in order to deepen my faith, it was also true that His enemy the devil could use the same circumstance to try to turn me away from Him. So, even in my pitiful state, I said aloud with great authority, 'And if you, Devil, have anything to do with this, then you can just go away! You have no business to taunt me. I am a child of God, my Father. In the name of the Lord Jesus, just go away!'

After that, I knew I must try to distract my wandering thoughts. My will-power was stretched to the limits, so alluring was the temptation to indulge in flights of imagination. I turned towards the shining metal panel beside my bed and switched on the radio. The sound of pop music was just fading. A disc-jockey started talking about the birth of a self-help group. He described how a couple had lost their baby. The doctors and nurses had been very kind, but all too soon, formal help had diminished. Their friends began to stop talking about their grief. Every form of help they had first received gradually stopped. But their need for care and comfort had continued.

The couple spoke for themselves. 'No amount of sympathy can stop you having to go through it,' they said. 'We had an aching void which was just not filled. We formed this group to help both ourselves and others in a similar unhappy position.'

The disc-jockey had sloppy music playing in the background. At the end of their 'moving story', as he put it, he added his own comments. 'You admire the courage of that couple, don't you, when you hear how they surmounted that kind of unhappiness?' he said sentimentally in his deep voice. Then the jangle of the next record boomed out and coaxed us all into carefree mood once again.

But they had had no choice!

I groaned into my pillow. It was neither romantic nor heroic, as he had made it seem. He was deceived. He saw only the areas in which they had been brave, but that was undoubtedly only one part of them. There would be another part which was crying out with the pain of their loss and their grief – just as I was crying out with mine as I listened.

He had made that couple's courage sound so glorious, but it would not have felt like that to them. They had probably felt totally unable to surmount their pain but, like me, how could they express their inability to do so? There is no option; no way out. Pain simply takes its victim over. It governs every move, almost like a machine which has been wound up and cannot stop until it has run its course. Under its influence and direction, I had often felt as if I just had to act out the awful mechanics of living in pain.

That couple would not want admiration because no amount of admiration counterbalances the heart's deep pain. What counted was a sense of being profoundly and tenderly cared for.

The attraction of my dream and memory of Elaine's visit to me in Edinburgh was that I had been comforted in my weakness. I had not had to fight to prove to her that I was brave. What I treasured in my memory was not her admiration, but compassion. She had comforted me in my passivity even before I had known that she was beside me. For once I had been 'caught' – unable to strive to show my courage. It was an unusual situation for me. I do not normally lie back and enjoy being comforted in weakness. To do so would feel like an indulgence in wallowing.

I turned over in bed, becoming drowsy with the radio's soft music. At last I slept, managing some escape, at least, from the heaviness of some of my thoughts.

I awoke gently this time, and tried to refresh myself for the conference once again. Standing under the shower in the elaborate hotel bathroom, I glanced up. The huge tinted mirror along one wall reflected my figure. The scar right down my abdomen seemed to glare back at me, prominent and red. At that moment I hated it, or rather, what it represented. I did not want to look. Quickly I wrapped my warm towel around me and began to dress.

Was I covering up the story of my pain? Did I 'cope' by hiding and suppressing what hurt? A particular phrase was ringing round in my head. So often I had heard people say, 'I don't know how you cope so marvellously . . .'

They are wrong. They take me for what I seem to be. I do not feel brave. I do not deserve admiration. Inside myself, I do not 'cope marvellously'. Whenever I have acute bouts of pain I have to struggle every minute, every hour, against crying out with the pain.

Throughout the whole day at the conference, I told no one of my inner desolation. I could not. What could I have said? There was a tedious history behind the inner pain I felt; how could anyone have understood it all?

In many ways, I could see why people said that I coped marvellously. I usually made myself appear normal, just as I was on that day; and I enjoyed doing so. But I also realised that throwing myself into life as I did prevented others from knowing my pain. If I had ever dared to share with people how I felt deep-down, they had invariably responded by saying, 'Jane, I never knew.'

That's it. They never really know. Pain is one's own. Others cannot know it all. Perhaps everyone is in pain, with their own pain, living in corporate isolation from one another. As the couple on the radio had said, 'Others may help you cope but in the end it's you that has to go through it.'

But I was a Christian, I reproached myself. God cares; He helps people through everything. I knew He was with me. How could I feel alone? I had received so much, and especially I had been supported and cared for by family and friends. Was I being ungrateful by feeling alone?

No. Matthew often assured me that he understood too well ever to accuse me of that. However close we were to one another, he was still on the sidelines. That, in a way, was the awful thing he had to bear: to watch, to care, but to be unable to take the pain away.

It was a long time afterwards that I talked this through with a very dear friend, Sarah. I was again very low with yet another episode of pain. 'I don't know what to say to you, Jane,' she said wretchedly. She did not know the relief she brought by simply holding questions with me instead of giving answers. She too had personal struggles which she needed to talk about. She had once found it particularly hard to hold on to her faith in the goodness of God. By sharing with one another about the times when we had each reached rock-bottom, we maybe brought to one another the presence of God Himself. Certainly it was something very precious.

'I feel terribly impotent, being so useless. But there's nothing I can do to help you.'

'You have helped,' I told her with conviction. 'You always make time to listen to me, without making me feel I'm a pest to you; and you find some encouragement without sounding empty. You will remain someone whom I can always trust at least to try to understand.'

It was true. One source of my heavy-heartedness was that I had met some Christians who had just shrugged their shoulders and said, 'Ah well, God knows best!' Their tone of voice was as quick and light-hearted as that nurse back in 1980, 'I heard you had your hyst.'. They had wanted to cheer me up by helping me to look on the bright side. But that just served to make me feel even more isolated because I was unable to ignore the pain and difficulties as they seemed to expect of me. That made the pain all the more lonely.

The loneliness of pain is perhaps its most excruciating aspect. It threatens to cut one off from others: and then to feel – worst of all – that one is abandoned by God Himself.

The paradox of Christian experience, however, is that death is always the gateway to life. Only in holding that truth did I find any ability to endure with patience.

8

'Endure with patience'

(2 Corinthians 1:6)

It is now ten years since I developed the first abscess following the original appendix operation. For those ten years I have yo-yo'd up and down, improving and relapsing, in and out of hospital. The time has been punctuated, but not relieved, by several major operations. And because little has changed outwardly, I now believe that God has called me to trust Him in darkness, to keep holding His hand even through the pain. He wants me to endure all things with Him.

Unfortunately I cannot simply disregard the pain, turning my back on suffering. The pain of peritonitis is not an optional extra, like a handbag which I can forget I am carrying. I only find it possible to live to the full by accepting life to the full – and that includes the pain. It means accepting the pain as part of me, part of being myself.

It is a hard path. There is a form of tiredness which those who are never ill do not know. Often I am too tired to read, too weary to knit, because the weight of my arms is too great. When I first waken from sleep I do not feel rested. I am still aware of the energy involved in lifting my head up to turn towards the clock. When the pain has been bad for some time, even breathing is tiring, such that I notice the effort in moving my chest, in opening my nostrils. Holding my arms and body together in its very existence feels too much. I often feel just too weary.

I wonder how long I will keep going in this sort of state, but somehow I am still here. I have to put conscious effort into making my muscles hold me standing upright. At times like these people must wonder why I don't concentrate well on a conversation! I feel as if I am on autopilot, forcing myself to walk, throwing one step after another, hoping I will not fall. Except, sometimes, I wish that I could fall, and let myself go completely, so that I could be free of feeling the weight of my body alive.

Time drags. I try to stop myself looking at the clock. But then suddenly I realise that more time has passed than I had guessed, and that seems a real blessing. I look forward to this painful phase of life being over.

But as 'this phase' of life goes on and on, I realise that pain is an integral part of my very living. I cannot wait for life to pass, but have to get down to living without watching the minutes ticking by. I cannot 'leave my pain at the cross' as some Christians would urge because, like the haunting poster of a boy in a wheel-chair, I could not walk away without it. Instead, I have to throw myself into making the most of my living in pain.

It's one thing to cope with the actual physical

endurance of my tummy being sore. That is at least contained in one place. But I loathe to see the effect rippling out to others, especially Matthew. It changes our relationship and sometimes I feel bitter that pain could succeed in its assaults upon something so precious. Until 1980 we never had any cross words or accusations against one another. Never.

But now we do. As always, it's the silly little things which precipitate inordinately heated responses. Instead of our giving one another strength to pull together against the suffering, all too easily things can somehow be turned around until we seem to be pulling against one another.

Not only do I reach the end of my tether with my own pain, but also Matthew does with his. It's as if he can last for so long watching me, feeling sympathetic and supportive towards me, before he reaches the limits of his unselfishness. Suddenly he will become aware of the cost to him and he will resent it. Not me: it. But I, watching him, feel that I am to blame. The pain is mine: could I not cope better so that he does not have to suffer as well?

The other day was a bad one in the midst of a week in which I was struggling simply to keep going. I was forcing myself round the house trying to do the basic chores. I had thought I was doing well until suddenly I heard the scraping noise of the smart wooden stools being kicked roughly under the breakfast bar.

'No butter!' came a heated expletive. Matthew was peeved. He likes butter on his toast in the morning: that is one of his treats to add sparkle to his 'keep-fit' régime.

I cringed. I felt accused, even although he had

been shouting at the situation, not at me personally. He had not known that I was just above the kitchen, slowly folding the washing from the airing cupboard. ('Keep on your feet, Jane. Don't dream about lying down. You must do this first.') Mind you, he was sufficiently angry that he probably wouldn't have minded that I heard.

My thoughts scanned over the past few days. Why was there no butter? How had I managed to let the old one run out without replacing it? I felt I had failed as Matthew's wife. A decent wife would ensure there was always enough butter for her husband's toast.

I remembered taking the empty butter dish over to the kitchen sink on the previous day. 'I must get a new packet from the freezer,' I had thought wearily as I took the brush to wash it. Then, 'later', I had added, thinking how far away the garage seemed at that moment. And later, of course, I had forgotten.

Now as I carried the neatly folded tea-towels into the kitchen I wondered what to say. This was my fault. I could not really blame pain for such a small thing. I had been lazy, then I had forgotten.

Matthew was not there. He was bashing about in his study now. Up on the wall, my shopping list was pinned as usual to the notice-board. Its whole page was filled with one word sprawled across it, 'B U T T E R'.

I felt very sorry for myself as I closed the drawer on my fresh supply of tea-towels. I thought of all that I had done over the past week, battling against how I had felt physically. And Matthew wasn't appreciative. All he was doing this morning was shouting at what I had failed to do.

In this sense of failure, feeling overwhelmed by pain, one of the worst things I can do is to look ahead. To endure patiently is much harder when there seems to be no time-limit to the pain. How quickly a feeling of desperation, a sort of claustrophobia, can come. I can rapidly become down-hearted as even slight episodes trigger off the memory of the depth of anguish associated with similar pain.

The most tedious aspect of chronic pain is its relentlessness, continuing on and on. I sometimes feel trapped by it; I am living in pain. I find myself saying, 'I cannot bear this.' I feel I could somehow cope if I could look forward to a day or a time when the pain will end, to console myself that I will soon feel better. Even the same afternoon can seem exhaustingly far ahead, and I think, 'I cannot get through until the children are in bed. I'll surely crack up before then!' But that is looking ahead.

Instead, I am trying to learn how to look only at the present. I should say to myself, 'You *are* bearing it, Jane', because pain is deceptive. It gives the impression that it will overwhelm for a long time. In practice, often just one day makes a huge difference. Within a few hours, unbearable pain can change and become almost-bearable. And of course, it is well known that pain is affected by morale. I am almost ashamed to confess that the most stupid little things, such as washing the dishes, can lift my morale enough to make the pain seem less intolerable.

Others can and do help. Matthew and I are frequently amazed by the sacrifices made by family and friends in order to help us, in whatever ways they choose. And yet, even that can have its own tension. People do what seems best; but that is not always what might help most.

Anyone who helps practically represents God helping me practically. One day a friend, Annegret, phoned to ask after me. I told her I was unwell again. This time, it was not so bad as to warrant admission to hospital, but I was in a lot of pain. Within two hours she had come round to the house, bringing food she had lovingly cooked for our family for the next week. She considered this to be meagre help in the face of such suffering; she would have preferred to take away my pain. Yet her visit to me was like a visit from God Himself saying, 'This is a sign that I care about you, even in the practicalities.'

However, on another occasion two people came unannounced with four meals between them. A big treat? Yes, except that all of it had previously been frozen and required to be eaten soon. To make matters more complicated, there was already food in our fridge which had to be cooked before it went stale. So while outwardly thanking the caring friends for their thoughtful gifts, Matthew was inwardly groaning. He still had to cook; he still had to think how he could best use the food; he still had to plan which dish had to be cooked most immediately. And, by the time he closed the door on those friends, the children were bored.

The sitting-room seemed uninviting and stale now. The glass-topped tables were smeared with grubby fingermarks. Shelves were cluttered with empty cups. Matthew dragged himself into the depressing scene, just in time to catch Philippa. Enjoying her new-found skill of crawling, she had just reached up for the brightly shining sugar-bowl.

As she grabbed clumsily for it, she knocked over a half-empty cup.

'Disgusting!' muttered Matthew under his breath, stomping heavily towards her. He lifted her exploring arms from patting the cold tea, now dripping on to the carpet, and carried her through to the kitchen to wash her. There, too, he was met with a mess. Cake tins were still left out from the folk who had brought the food. He snapped one lid closed but, before he could put it away, there was a sudden wail from the sitting-room.

Angus had become bored after enduring visitors one after another. Each had excluded him from their discussions of 'important' things. At three years old he could have made his own contribution to the conversation about Mummy's sore tummy. He would have enjoyed explaining that she had had a tube into her 'bud vessel' which he thought looked like a train going along a railway line. But people had not expected him to converse, so he had not. Instead he had set up an assault course, jumping from a wooden chair on to a huge floor cushion. It had amused him for a while, until one jump when he had bumped his head on the bookshelf by mistake.

Matthew raced through. Tears flowed freely, but more out of boredom than physical pain. Angus wanted to let Matthew know that he wanted as much time with Daddy as others got. Grown-ups somehow had the knack of demanding attention immediately: when they rang the doorbell, Matthew answered it and there ensued a conversation. Angus had to come second to the doorbell or the telephone. He was still too little to have learned how sociably to demand time from Matthew's busy life, except by a huge wail.

Matthew sat cradling Angus, stroking his hair. He admired the assault course and soon they were both laughing about the bumped head. 'Bumps are inevitable if we do dangerous things to enjoy life,' they agreed. 'Pain is worthwhile when we've had fun.'

Upstairs in bed, I heard it all.

'Would you like a story?' Matthew suggested to Angus. Stories were a good opportunity for a quietly intimate time together. That would entertain both him and Philippa. 'Oooh!' came the enthusiastic reply, and Angus ran to choose a book.

But Matthew's voice did not hold the same enthusiasm now. His reading was mechanical today. His mind was not with Thomas the Tank Engine. It was in the study, thinking about his work. He needed space to think. How best could he encourage those four mums to help with a new pram service in church? How were the three teenagers coping whose mother died recently? What could he do to catch the interest of the children in tomorrow's school assembly? That was work. His work. Amusing children was not real work: not in the same, fulfilling way. How could he do justice to God in his work this week without time? Time to think? And pray?

The story over, and Philippa contentedly emptying a fresh box of toys, Matthew planned he might snatch a few moments to think on his own. He began to gather together the empty mugs. 'You just carry on while I try to tidy up a bit,' he suggested.

But Angus was still bored; no suggestion caught his imagination now. 'May I watch television? *My* programme?' he asked, recognising the distinctive set of the clock's hands at 4.00 p.m. for the start of children's television.

Matthew was thwarted from carrying through the dishes. He turned round, frustrated from his plans and cross that Angus had succeeded in squeezing a little bit more of his attention. A little bit more, and a little bit more. If it wasn't friends calling, it was Angus, or the telephone, or Philippa. And he hadn't been upstairs to see me for a while . . . me, quietly shedding a tear after hearing their earlier conversation. 'Pain is worthwhile when we've had fun . . .' they had said. What about when it prevents us having fun in the first place, I was wondering? I was glad Matthew had not come up. I would only have been yet another burden on him. He was suffering enough already.

'Well, it depends what the TV programme is,' Matthew conceded reluctantly. But already Angus had raced over to press the switch. 'Paddington!' he cried with glee. 'Mummy lets me watch this.'

Matthew trudged through to the kitchen. He felt trampled on, taken-over; as if he had no place to make decisions any more. He was ruled by the ricocheting effect of my pain.

Upstairs I could not settle. I was no longer resting, except physically. My mind was in turmoil. I could understand some of Matthew's pain and I wanted to help. I was sorry for him, yet also afraid of his anger. I knew he might fly at someone – maybe at the children, maybe at me. I knew it would not be meant personally if he did. Just as I sometimes have to bear more physical pain

than I feel able, now he was bearing too much
emotional pain.

Does it seem ungrateful of Matthew to be burdened by others' help? Therein lies yet another
source of tension for him. He knows he must
only be grateful to others for all help offered.
He would hate to hurt them by suggesting that
their goodwill could be better channelled. So he
bears more. Silently.

Inevitably, he feels a reaction. I want him to
be free to express his reaction, and not to try to
suppress everything, bottling up his feelings inside
himself. He's inclined to do that anyway, having
been taught at boarding school that it is 'good'
not to show unpleasant emotions. So strongly has
this been ingrained in him that he automatically
feels guilty when he finds anger within himself.
At that stage he either denies it, or falls silent
(easily mistaken for moodiness) as he tussles within
himself.

On the one hand Matthew wants to weep for me
and shout out against the apparent injustice that he
should see me suffer more than many others; on the
other hand he has this strong inbuilt sense that he
should be able to cope. This is made even stronger
whenever he recognises God's hand working even
within all our suffering. If God is so clearly in
it, then surely Matthew should be able to come
through with a glowing Christian serenity?

And across the two threads, he has the practical
everyday chores during my crises, such as keeping
the children happy and finding the next meal
– things which he is not accustomed to doing
simultaneously.

One of the ways in which other people help us

to endure with patience is by encouraging us in every way, including in prayer. Not the insistent kind of prayer which tells God what to do, but the quiet waiting upon Him together. I was helped not only by the direct effect of prayer on myself, but also because I could see how much Matthew was strengthened and made more peaceful by it.

Every Monday for about eighteen months while Matthew was at theological college, about a dozen friends joined together to pray. They were precipitated into meeting like this in 1980 while I was so critically ill, but they did not give up as soon as the crisis had passed. Even other very worthwhile demands on their time did not make them cease. For Matthew and myself, their faithfulness was an enormous encouragement. For themselves, they became convinced that those who pray benefit as much as the one being prayed for.

There was one such evening, just before Easter 1980, when the group was drawn to one particular verse which has continued to be a great source of strength. They had been silent for a long time as they simply lifted me to God in their minds. A stillness came upon them, gentle yet powerful. Then the quietness was broken by three different people.

'I've a tune repeating itself over and over in my ears,' said Peter.

'I've a picture in my mind,' said Anne.

'I've a verse which I cannot get out of my head,' was John's contribution. 'But I'm not sure where to find it.'

'Maybe someone else will know?' Alastair was leading that evening. 'Tell us what it is.'

The words came easily as John spoke the verse:

'The steadfast love of the Lord never ceases; his mercies never come to an end.' Little could he guess how much his trust in those words would be tested the following years, with the long and continuing illness of his wife, Sadie.

'That's amazing that you should quote that verse!' exclaimed Peter. 'Because the tune which came to me was from the song with those very words; they come from Lamentations 3.' He picked up his guitar and everyone joined in quietly to sing the song about God's steadfast love.

After it was finished, it was Anne's turn. 'The picture in my mind fits in with both the verse and the song,' she said. 'I can see a crocus, a beautiful crocus. The outer leaves are curled around the fragile petals of the flower. It's like loving hands protecting something, or someone, very precious.'

The room was silent again while everyone reflected on what had been shared. They all marvelled at the one message of assurance and love, given so clearly in three different ways, but at the same time. Gradually the hush became diffused with praise, in prayer and in song, that God's Spirit should so graciously be among them.

I had been too tired to go to this particular meeting, but as soon as Matthew returned to me later in hospital I could see that he was radiant. He was filled and surrounded by an aura of peace; not a passive, 'Let happen what will happen', but a peace which was somehow very powerful.

The group did not quote this verse glibly, as a quick means of explaining the pain away without entering into our suffering. The words were actually written by Jeremiah among shouts of anguish to the

Lord, 'He [God] has driven me away and made me walk in darkness rather than light' (Lam. 3:2). Yet Jeremiah's hope returned whenever he remembered that God's steadfast love remained even in the depths of suffering. 'Though he brings grief, he will show compassion . . .' (Lam. 3:32).

When my own trust crumbles and questioning turns into doubt, it is not only my physical strength which fails. I weaken emotionally and spiritually, too, and have to depend on others' help. Even though I was not there myself, that special evening in 1980 gave me a profound trust in God's steadfast love – no matter what. Through others waiting on God, as if on my behalf, I feel that Lamentations 3 is a special source of comfort.

In order to keep the significance of this verse alive within me, I must be patient. To look ahead is to lose patience. To look for a time-limit is to lose patience. To demand an explanation of God's purpose through it all is to lose patience. I have had to learn how to grit my teeth and force myself to get through. But that is not the sort of patience that God wants for me. He wants me to learn patience with joy.

I remember reading the book of Colossians while feeding Philippa as a baby. Because I was then caring for the two children, time was short and I was trying to cram my prayer time and Bible-reading into the brief peacefulness when Angus was at playgroup. The sun streamed into our quiet sitting-room, almost as a picture of God's presence illumining what I was reading.

It was the first time that I had noticed the phrase, 'patience with joy' (Col. 1:11 RSV). That was part of Paul's prayer for the Christians he was addressing.

'Oooh, Lord,' I prayed as soon as I noticed it. 'I'd like patience with joy.' I realised that a lot of the time my so-called 'patience' was more like long-suffering; that I lacked the joy which comes from God's own patience. 'Please give me patience with joy,' I prayed.

I stopped for a moment. I did not hear God's physical voice, but in the pause after my prayer a new thought came to me. It was as if God were talking. 'Patience and joy are not gifts. They are fruit; part of the fruit of the Holy Spirit. Like fruit on a tree, they grow, slowly but surely. They cannot be stuck on with glue.'

My momentary excitement waned a little. I realised that my prayer for patience and joy as a gift was inappropriate. If I wanted them, I had to be prepared to steep myself more fully in God's Spirit, so that He could bring forth the fruit as a natural consequence of my life in Him.

I adjusted my prayer. 'Help me to live more closely to You – more *in* You than *with* You, and I'll still look to You to make patience and joy grow out of my life.'

I felt quite subdued as I realised what my prayer actually meant. Patience grows from endurance; endurance from suffering. To pray for patience was very different from praying for the pain to end. It meant opening myself to God, whether or not the pain continued. Indeed it meant accepting the possibility that the pain could continue, in order to bear fruit – God's fruit.

There would be no easy path to joy, either. To some extent, joy grows out of sorrow. To ask for the fruit of the Holy Spirit to be seen in my life was to accept God's hand completely. In His great wisdom He seems to have chosen to teach me His path to joy through suffering.

It seemed, and still does seem, to be a daunting road. I only keep on the apparently endless trudge of carrying on, by being encouraged. I need to be affirmed that I *am* in the Lord's hands, even when it looks as if He has let go of me.

To endure with patience sounds tremendously heroic; in reality it is tough and unexciting. Trapped in the midst of the pain, I am unable to stand back objectively in the way that onlookers can. To endure patiently seems so endlessly hard; it drives one even to the point of despair.

It is paradoxical that, when I have felt thus, God has been reflected in me. I greatly value the comments of my friends whose perspective is different from my own. Elaine's words are but one example. She wrote, 'Your courage and trust in the face of such suffering and ongoing discouragement cannot help but witness to the glory of God.'

In the face of all that I have to endure, this is my encouragement. I can be a light to those around me. I can please God within my suffering. I can even have a ministry in suffering.

One letter which I will always treasure is from Geoff, who came to see me when I felt weary and spent. I had no idea at the time that I had anything to offer in life, to God or to others. Such a knowledge would have been sufficient encouragement for me to stop feeling so low and useless. Yet Geoff wrote:

Thank you so much for our time together which

gave me so much. It is a joy to be with you, and to see maybe something which you cannot: the quiet joy of Christ radiating through the daily painful and victorious cross that He has placed upon your frail shoulders. You may not see this 'quiet joy' that I mention, but I can see it and have seen it before . . . Christ lives within you, and what we see in you is an unending limit of endurance and faithfulness which is possible only in Him.

We can be very slow to encourage one another; yet each person who suffers desperately needs to be encouraged. He needs to know that, although much of the action in his life is completely curtailed by pain, that life is bearing fruit. It is worthwhile. It is the beginning of the journey towards healing through pain.

9

Healing through pain

Much has happened since this book was first published in 1987.

Physically I continued bumping along, in and out of hospital. The problem was not primarily one of infection, but of low-grade inflammation. However, I had had so many major operations that bits of my abdomen had stuck together, forming adhesions. Instead of everything moving about freely, movement caused me pain because the adhesions got tugged. This was only sore. Occasionally, however, the situation became more threatening. The adhesions could twist, causing an acute obstruction in my intestine. I was in agony, then, and vomiting exhaustingly. I would have to be admitted to hospital in the hope that the twist would settle with various medical treatments, and in the knowledge that if it didn't, I would need yet more surgery.

It was an uneasy waiting game on every occasion. If the surgeon had waited too long to operate, the

intestine could have ruptured with fatal results. If
he had been too hasty, I may have been subjected
to major surgery which I might not have survived.
Either way, my life was lived on a knife-edge.

I began to write my own form of psalms, or letters
to God. Concentration was short-lived; so too were
all my written prayers. They were starkly honest.
I felt I had nothing to offer to God, but I began
to learn to offer even that. One such poem was
written in bed as I felt myself wince at every breath.
I was caught between two impossible opposites:
simultaneously longing for tenderness yet being
unable to let even Matthew close enough for me
to receive just that.

> Do not kiss me now
> Do not come too close
> It's every breath which I must breathe
> Now
> and again
> Now . . .
>
> > I hear a groan with each one:
> > Is that my voice?
> > I do not mean to grunt.
> > If I hold my breath
> > Does that help?
> > . . . I cannot.
> > My body's past such pride.
> > Instead I'll delay each one . . .
>
> Just stroke me now:
> My arm
> My forehead
> Run your fingers through my hair.
> Without words,

Soothe me
Reach me
in this world with no words
this world where tears will not flow
for anguish

Ah! Staccato stabbing
Pain piercing
Throbbing
Punctuated by these cries
Suppressed
but not silenced.

Would that this were singing
and not a cry of distress!
Oh my God! my God . . .

Accept each groan
each involuntary groan
and make it into
a song for You.

I did not hear my groaning as a song for God; nor, indeed, my prayers. If I was honest, I was bored to hear them and I wondered if God wasn't bored, too. However, I had no choice. I either gave Him all I could, or I hugged my hurts to myself. Furthermore I did not doubt His power to transform and I found that leaning my weight on Him offered great hope. In writing (or praying) thus I discovered that instead of these being moments of my reaching out to God, the dynamic was in fact His reaching out to me.

This may sound rather grand; in fact it felt pitiful. Although I was aware of my relationship with God plumbing ever greater depths, that spiritual reward did not seem worth the cost. I could not see any worth in any of what was happening: not in my pain, nor my writing, nor my hope. It seemed to be all useless. My life seemed such a waste.

During the spring of 1988 a very ordinary scene from my window seemed to depict a parable of our situation.

I was sitting comfortably strewn across two bean-bags, gazing out to the three huge beech trees which stood majestically on the far side of our garden wall. The sun had risen quite high, and against its silvery brightness some dark rooks were silhouetted black and menacing.

'Those rooks are terribly destructive,' I remarked to Matthew as he came through. 'Look at them! They're pulling those poor trees to pieces.'

As we watched, no fewer than four rooks worked on different parts of the trees. They pecked with their beaks and stamped with their feet, clawing determinedly at the twigs until they had cut off the piece they wanted. Some of the twigs seemed enormous, and I was amazed the birds were able to fly at all carrying such cumbersome pieces.

Matthew was more philosophical than I. 'I was just thinking how clever it all is,' he mused. 'If you look carefully, they only take the bits which come off easily. It's a very neat way of the weak parts of the tree being removed, which actually has the effect of keeping the whole thing growing more strongly.'

He was right.

And that was only a part of the whole picture. The rooks were not purposeless. Their tearing-down was not futile. Elsewhere, of course, they were building their nests. But the trees where the new nests were being built, although only half a mile away, were out of my sight. From my bean-bags, I could see only the destructive tearing-down.

That morning I knew how easy it was – and is – to mourn when we see tearing-down; to fail to see that that is part of building. It cannot, or should not, be separated from building-up. For without the tearing-down of twigs there would be no building of nests.

This is why I remained uncomfortable to talk or to write about the destructive element of suffering. We may feel only brokenness; we may never see what is being built up. But that does not – or should not! – matter. Indeed, I knew that, just as the rooks' new nests were not even in the same tree as these ones where twigs were being torn off, perhaps the harvest from my pain might never be visible in my life here, but it could yet be to come. Or perhaps others could see what I could not.

In the summer of 1989, I entered another severe phase of illness and I became acutely ill once more. The consultant, a skilled and gentlemanly surgeon, called Matthew into his rooms immediately after examining me. It was plain from his whole demeanour that he was bearing bad news. He had found my blood-pressure low, my pulse-rate high. He explained with a sense of some urgency that the infection had returned once again: I had acute peritonitis. I was weak and gravely ill. However, although normally he would have operated on the suspected abscess before it burst, he feared I might not survive another operation. His voice, always calm, spoke with particular tenderness.

The treatment he chose was less traumatic, more conservative than surgery, consisting of drips and injections while my condition was monitored intensively. During the following few days my life simply ebbed away. Friends who came to visit me, who had been astonished at the fighting spirit they had seen helping me through bad times before, now saw me and were shocked. This was the most traumatic time of all for Matthew. He could see a special peace settle over me, increasingly, as my hold on to life weakened. He was the one left struggling, fighting back the tears, needing the grace to let go of me but not feeling that grace to be as evident as he wanted.

I wrote many more psalms. In the small hours of the morning I poured out my soul before God – and once again, it was as if God was pouring out His soul before me. That bed in Fazakerley hospital became holy ground. The overwhelming hallmark of all that I wrote is not my weakness but God's transformation.

I recall one particular night when Matthew and I had said goodbye to one another. We were serene rather than sombre; we were both held in an embrace of God's peace. I watched Matthew leave and saw his closeness to tears as he struggled to release his hold on my mortal life. And as I prayed for him through the following long hours, the picture which came to me was of Jesus transforming water into wine. Weakly grasping a pencil, little by little as I lay there that night I wrote to Matthew:

*   *   *

Do not weep
when my body will rest at last

Do not weep
when its loud demands
are silenced at last

Do not weep
when writhing has ceased
and I can lie quietly
beside still waters

Or if you do:
  if tears well up
  in the chalice of your soul
Give God your tears

And let Him change them
into rich wine
consecrated to Him

We knew, both Matthew and I, that we could give God absolutely nothing except miserable, watery wretchedness. And as I lay through that night, aware of the burden of my every breath, I found the beauty of hope. This can have been little less than a touch of God. Quite unbidden I knew that God could take our supposed nothingness and replace it with the richness of Himself. I knew, too, that He could take what is transparent – feelings – and suffuse them with what has substance – faith. Just like water into wine.

Physically I did not find 'rest at last'. My body's loud demands were not silenced and, however much my soul had been stilled, my body's writhing did not cease. Instead I gradually began to improve until I was out of danger, if not out of pain. Under the care of that tender and competent consultant, the infection cleared and I became better enough to be discharged from the ward. I had turned the corner.

Home again, I slid back to the practised régime of gritting my teeth and shutting my eyes in order to carry on through life. It was a hard few months which followed. My priority was to give myself to the children as best I could. All my energy was directed into them – into providing meals, and into listening to them and laughing with them in between times. If I had to lie down, I did so where we could still have fun together. Family life was very full and healthy – perhaps the more so because of its high priority.

Other people's help was invaluable: they cooked casseroles for us, bought shopping for us, they cleaned the house and ironed the clothes for us. When I look back I see what a privilege this all was. Perhaps at the time the need for help was so great that I accepted it all as if it were my right. Only when I stand back do I recognise the grace which must have been given to so many for them all to pull together in this way, and to do it without looking to me for thanks.

My prayers – to my shame – kept coming back to me telling God how dreadful I felt, and begging Him to be involved. It was as if I was using prayer as a weapon in my battle against the weariness and against the fear that I might lose. I would ask for strength, for courage to keep going, for hope despite the disappointment of discovering each day that the tedious burden had not been lifted. However, I began to write down what I was saying to God, along with the psalms. The more I read over my prayers, the more I realised the blinkers I had on when I tried to use prayer as a weapon. It was, instead, more like a window – a window to myself, and a window to God.

Gradually, gradually, prayer became less of an event in my day and more of a pair of spectacles which changed the colour and hue of every part of life. It was less of a quest for God to involve Himself more actively in me; more of a means for me to learn how to involve myself more actively in Him.

Then suddenly, April 1990. I had fought for so long on this knife-edge between chronic pain and acute illness, I had dulled my senses. I did not know when I was so near to the edge that I was about to crash down.

'Don't worry!' I assured the doctor one day when she suggested admitting me to hospital. She was a locum for our general practitioner and I felt she was more alarmed than was necessary. 'I'm not as ill as you think. All I need is pain relief. Look, I know! I've lived with this; I know when things are really bad and that's not now!'

Little did I know . . .

I owe my life to two things. First, the doctor did not believe me and she insisted upon admitting me to hospital immediately. Secondly, Matthew asked a friend from church, Jenny, to drive me into hospital since he really could not face it. Not only was Jenny a doctor herself but also she brought her husband Andrew who was a specialist in anaesthetics and intensive care of patients.

How differently events could have turned out!

How close to death can one go and yet be brought back from the brink? On the way to hospital I lost consciousness. Andrew could not find my pulse: both he and Jenny thought I would be a 'DOA' (dead on arrival) when eventually they arrived at the hospital. Quickly they switched direction in order to get me to the nearest hospital as fast as possible; it happened to be where Andrew worked. With their help I was rushed in and was given the emergency treatment I needed.

All that night I hung on to life by a thread, my blood-pressure falling lower and lower until at about three o'clock in the morning – that low hour before dawn – my kidneys stopped functioning. I remember the thud of absolute horror when suddenly I realised the significance of what was happening. I was being 'specialed' with a nurse continuously monitoring my breathing, my heart-beat, and watching the various tubes and oxygen all keeping me going. With alarm she noticed that my catheter had stopped draining. She called the second Sister; they fiddled to check the tubes but, no, there was no mistake. My kidneys had stopped functioning.

Quickly they called the registrar.

'I want you to tell me honestly, how d'you feel?' he asked.

All night I had been fighting by denial; trying stupidly to persuade myself that I would become better if I dismissed the suffering. Now I was trapped: held, really, by honesty, but it felt like a trap because I knew I could no longer escape. The doctor's ability to hold the pain without diminishing it gave me permission to face the awfulness of what was happening as perhaps I never had before.

I had to speak through my oxygen mask. 'Well, actually,' I stammered, 'I don't feel very well.'

The registrar buried his tired face in his hands.

'Not very well,' he repeated slowly. He looked up.'You are bloody ill, Jane! OK?'

The moment of humour passed; he ordered further steps to try to stop me falling irretrievably down the ravine which was opening up with widening yawn. But my temperature dropped; my pulse raced. Still conscious, I was literally watching my body cease. And this time I felt no peace. No calm assurance of God being with me. I had been overtaken by a terrible mistake which had caught me unawares. It was like a thief which had crept in unseen and was getting away with stealing my life before it could be stopped.

This time the restraints on operating were cast aside. However dangerous it might be, the surgeon decided the following morning that he could not allow the situation to continue. He asked Matthew to come to his office so he could speak confidentially.

'You can't!' Matthew told him desperately. 'We've been told before, most recently last summer, that it would be too dangerous to operate on Jane.'

'It would be too dangerous for us not to.'

'She may not survive!'

'She won't survive if we don't.'

Matthew was distraught. There was only one thin hope among so much grim news and he clung to that. Andrew, our friend and consultant anaesthetist, assured Matthew that he would find the best anaesthetist in the area for the operation. He swapped his own list in order to do it himself.

Matthew talks of three miracles which followed. The first was that, despite my weakness, I survived the invasion of surgery and an anaesthetic. The second was that the surgeons were able to divide the offending adhesions. Whereas previously when I had been opened up there had been too many adhesions for the surgeons to operate, this time there were fewer. Whereas previously my bladder had been stuck so firmly to the abdominal wall the surgeon could not distinguish one tissue from another and had had to leave the mess stuck together for fear of puncturing the bladder, this time the adhesions were clearly defined and my bladder was separated. Two specific bands of adhesions were identified as having been the culprit for most, if not all, of the pain, and they were skilfully released.

The third miracle is that I began to improve. And what began continued and I became better than I had done after any other operation. For twelve months or so we had no need for a doctor. Then, and only once, Matthew and I were able to recognise the signs accurately and deal with them instantly. We called the doctor promptly and I was admitted to hospital safely without tortuous side-issues getting in the way. I was in hospital for only about forty-eight hours and felt bruised for only about a week.

Now, nearly three years on, progress is continuing. I feel as if I am going from strength to strength. I am working every day (writing) and am engaged with life. I am playing tennis. Last summer I even went on an outward-bound holiday enjoying ridiculously strenuous activities such as abseiling and rock-climbing, canoeing and surfing, hiking on foot, on mountain-bike, and on horseback. The week represented a celebration of life, life in its fullness physically, and it was exhilarating fun.

I close my eyes and give praise almost daily for the physical release God has given me. I hope the physical horror is past and that I never, never have to face such agonies as I've been through again. I hope the last operation proves to have been the final one.

But in thanking God for my new strength, I also – tremblingly – must thank Him for the weakness. My physical well-being could be a distraction from what I believe healing to be. If we count 'success' – or freedom from what we find unpleasant – if we say that that is the same as 'healing', then we may be cutting ourselves off from embracing the profound depths of God.

I am coming to believe that an important part of healing is to be broken, and to reflect God in that brokenness. In writing this chapter I can see that I am beginning a whole book about healing and pain, and the vital integration of suffering and freedom, failure and success.

Having written of my health I am afraid, selfishly, of people rejoicing to the point of causing hurt – not only to me, by overlooking the cost of the pain, but more importantly to God, by misrepresenting Him. We diminish God's work if we will only rejoice in so-called success.

Every day I am aware of the persistent loss which is a legacy of my journey. I still need to rest – sleep – for two hours every afternoon. Even then, occasionally tiredness consumes whole weeks at a time, sapping me of vivacity and humour and life in its fullness.

In the wake of serious illness, tiredness can feel more like a shut-down of the body. Suddenly, unbidden, near the end of shopping or in the middle of an interesting exhibition for example, I will feel the weight of utter exhaustion. I feel wretched and continue to do so until I have rested thoroughly. Inevitably, whenever this happens, I remember why I am particularly susceptible to such tiredness and I am back to being thrust into an ambulance, into hospital, on a trolley and surrounded either by bustle or by the silent tension of intensive care.

It would be foolish for Matthew or myself to forget that symptoms could return any time. Medically this would be no surprise. And then, of course, we would feel all the more isolated if people were so busy rejoicing about my improvement that they could not see that 'healing' does not mean 'healed'.

There are other costs to pay in the present. I do not have the stamina to go back to nursing and I would dearly love to. I was unable to carry my own children physically during pregnancy and I would dearly love to have done, even although we adopted each one from within hours of their birth.

Thus I cannot 'count my blessings' to the point of ignoring what has gone before. Humanly speaking, that cost has been too high. As I write this, I know I am laying myself open to condemnation (from myself if not from others) because I cannot muster the same rejoicing as some Christians may want.

But more important than any fears for myself, I do not want to fuel the myths about God Himself and about what healing is. To 'put the pain years all behind' is a way of disregarding some very precious truths about Him.

I want to resist the so-called optimism which empties my experience of its awfulness. I believe God does not want to confine Himself to areas where He is recognised – in visible healing. God is with us in our pain as much as He is in our rejoicing. His light shines in our darkness as well as in our day. The place from which we want to escape may be the very place where He is waiting to be found. When we have lost sight of Him altogether we fear Him to have withdrawn; in fact He has embedded Himself in the darkness within us where we fear even to look.

In a subtle way, rejoicing can be a way of dismissing pain, and I believe that by avoiding pain we can avoid healing. We cannot speak of healing if we will not speak of pain. Our Lord carried His scars into Resurrection – and so do I.

There's a score across the sky, there
Where an aeroplane's just been
Cutting it and marring it
Slicing it in two

There's a score across my abdomen
Where surgeons' knives have been
Cutting me and marring me
Slicing me in two

There's a score across my life, Lord
Where deepest hurts have been
I am so marred
and cut apart
in many, many ways

      The trail above me's fading now
      Blown across the sky
      The scar across my abdomen
      is fading with the years
      But the scar across my life, Lord,
      Never can be swept away

Save me from seeing only hurt:
Show me Your hand as well.
For with one touch
You leave your mark
Changing me, not marring me
Leading me
to You.